Fermenting & Pickling Essentials

Time-Honored Techniques for Long-Term Storage

Lucas Bennett

Table of Contents

INTRODUCTION

The age-old crafts of pickling and fermentation have come back into vogue as beloved customs, providing access to both superior cuisine and food preservation in a time of ease and fast-paced living. Welcome to "Fermenting & Pickling Essentials: Time-Honored Techniques for Long-Term Storage."

This book is your pass to the fascinating realm of food preservation using tried-and-true techniques that have been handed down through the ages. We will take a trip through these pages that goes beyond the transient quality of fresh ingredients so you can enjoy their flavors and nutritional value for months or even years to come.

You might wonder, why pickle and ferment? Fermented and pickled foods provide a varied and incredibly gratifying range of flavors and sensations, even beyond their ability to prolong shelf life. These culinary treats can take meals to new levels, whether you're enjoying the umami depth of kimchi or the acidic crunch of dill pickles. We will demystify these traditional methods as we dig into the realm of pickling and fermentation, including the science behind them, the tools you'll need, and the wide range of materials you can use. We'll study the techniques for making perfectly crisp pickles, learn how to make probiotic-rich sauerkraut, and venture beyond veggies to the worlds of fermented beverages, condiments, and dairy products.

This book is your all-inclusive guide, whether you're a beginner looking to take on your first fermentation journey or an experienced pickle maker trying to broaden your repertory. Get ready to explore the Fermenting &

Pickling Essentials world, taste the magic of preservation, and discover the flavors of tradition.

CHAPTER I

Getting Started

The Tools and Equipment You'll Need

Having the correct tools and equipment is critical when experimenting with pickling and fermenting. For these traditional methods of food preservation to be successful and safe, a particular set of items is needed. This section will review the different tools and equipment you'll need to start pickling and fermenting.

The key to successfully pickling and fermenting food is cleanliness and accuracy. You will need food-grade plastic or glass containers with airtight lids first and foremost. For this use, mason jars, crocks, or fermentation vessels are useful. These containers offer a safe haven for your pickling or fermenting components, letting the released gases during fermentation flow out while keeping dangerous bacteria out.

Fermentation weights are essential to keep vegetables covered in brine or other liquids during fermenting. A good fermentation is ensured by keeping your ingredients below the liquid's surface, which also inhibits mold growth and spoiling. Options for weights range from simple sterilized rocks to specially designed ceramic weights.

Precise ingredient proportions require accurate measuring equipment, such as measuring cups and kitchen scales. Recipes frequently specify amounts of water, salt, or other ingredients to keep the proper balance for fermentation. Accurate measurement equipment can help you produce consistent, trustworthy results.

A thermometer is another essential piece of equipment, particularly for people new to fermenting. It's critical to keep the fermentation process at the right temperature. Most fermentations are optimally conducted between 60 and 75°F (15 and 24°C). You can monitor and regulate the temperature with a high-quality kitchen thermometer, creating an ideal atmosphere for the fermentation process.

Airlocks and fermentation lids that are safe for food are essential additions to your toolbox. The devices keep air and other impurities out of the container while allowing the gases generated during fermentation to escape. There are many different fermentation lids and airlocks designs, ranging from basic water-filled airlocks to more sophisticated one-way valve systems. The type of fermentation you're doing and your personal tastes will determine which one is best for you.

A set of sharp knives, cutting boards, and other culinary instruments are necessary for chopping and prepping items. When it comes to pickling and fermenting fruits, vegetables, and other ingredients, the quality of your tools can make a big difference in how quickly and efficiently you work.

You'll need non-iodized salt for brining. Using salt devoid of iodine is crucial since iodine can impede fermentation. Popular options include kosher salt, sea salt, and pickling salt. Try experimenting to achieve diverse flavors in your pickled foods since different types of salt could have slightly different flavor profiles.

The quality of your water is essential to the success of your fermentations. Use water without chlorine if possible, as chlorine may impede the growth of good bacteria necessary for fermentation. It might be required to use a chlorine-removing filter or leave your tap water exposed for a whole day to dechlorinate it.

One often-ignored but essential equipment for fermentation is a kitchen timer. Temperature and recipe factors affect how long a recipe takes to ferment. Using a timer can prevent over-fermenting your food, which can result in unfavorable textures and tastes.

Identifying supplies, including detachable labels and waterproof markers, are be handy for monitoring your fermentations. Having each batch properly labeled guarantees that you know when it was started, which can help you keep your process organized and efficient.

In addition to these essential tools, optional equipment can enhance your pickling and fermenting experience. For example, cabbage pounders help pack vegetables tightly into kimchi or sauerkraut containers. You can ensure your fermentations are safe for long-term storage by keeping an eye on their acidity with pH testing meters or strips. Once your fermented and pickled goods are complete, you'll need storage containers and jars for the finished products.

In conclusion, the equipment and tools needed for pickling and fermenting are simple but essential to the success of your cooking projects. Every tool used to create delectable and securely kept goods has a specific function, from weights and containers to thermometers and labeling. Investing in the appropriate tools and maintaining a clean and controlled environment will prepare you to dive into the rich and flavorful world of pickling and fermenting. So, grab your equipment and start learning the craft of food preservation.

Selecting the Right Ingredients

The quality and variety of ingredients used are crucial to the art of pickling and fermenting. When preserving fruits, vegetables, or other food items, the selection of ingredients greatly influences the end product's flavor, consistency, and success. In this section, we'll look at the essential factors in choosing the best ingredients for pickling and fermenting.

Freshness is one of the first factors to consider while choosing ingredients. Freshness is crucial since it influences the flavor and consistency of your fermented or pickled items. Use ingredients that are at their ripest possible point; underripe or overripe fruit can lead to less-than-ideal results. Local ingredients are usually fresher and more flavorful than those that have traveled great distances, so try to acquire them whenever you can.

The quality of your water is another vital factor to consider. Water makes up a significant portion of your pickling or fermenting solution, so it's essential to use water that is clean and free of contaminants. In fermentation, the growth of helpful bacteria can be inhibited by chlorinated tap water. Use a chlorine-removing filter or leave tap water uncovered for a full day to allow the chlorine to evaporate. As an alternative, if well or spring water is readily available and of high quality, you can utilize it in bottled form.

The type of salt you choose is critical for pickling and fermenting. Non-iodized salt is essential, as iodine can interfere with the fermentation process. Common options include pickling salt, sea salt, and kosher salt. Each type of salt may have slightly different mineral profiles and flavors, so experimenting with other salts can lead to unique taste experiences in your pickled and fermented creations.

When selecting vegetables or fruits for pickling and fermenting, opt for those that are firm and free from any visible signs of spoilage or decay. When feasible, choose for organic vegetables because it is less likely to have pesticides or chemical residues that may interfere with fermentation. Washing and thoroughly inspecting your ingredients before use is a standard practice to remove any dirt, insects, or unwanted contaminants.

Variety is the spice of life in the world of pickling and fermenting. Don't limit yourself to common vegetables like cucumbers and cabbage. Explore various vegetables, fruits, and even proteins to discover new and exciting flavors. Popular options include carrots, beets, radishes, onions, apples, and even fish or shrimp for traditional dishes like fish sauce. The possibilities are endless, and experimenting with different ingredients can lead to unique and delightful results.

Consider the seasonality of your chosen ingredients. Certain vegetables and fruits are best suited for pickling and fermenting during specific times of the year when they are at their peak freshness and flavor. For example, cucumbers are ideal for pickling in the summer months when they are abundant and crisp. Planning your pickling and fermenting projects around seasonal ingredients can yield the best results and connect you more closely to the rhythms of nature.

Spices and seasonings are the final layer of flavor in your pickled and fermented creations. From garlic and dill to coriander seeds and chili flakes, the right combination of spices can elevate your pickles and ferments to new heights. Experiment with different spice blends to find the flavors that suit your taste preferences. Be sure to use high-quality spices and herbs, as their freshness and potency will significantly impact the final product.

In conclusion, selecting the right ingredients for pickling and fermenting is vital in creating flavorful and safely preserved foods. Essential considerations include freshness, water quality, salt type, and ingredient variety. By paying attention to these factors and exploring the rich array of options available, you can craft pickled and fermented foods that are delicious and reflective of your creativity and appreciation for the art of food preservation. So, embrace the diversity of ingredients at your disposal, and let your culinary adventures in pickling and fermenting begin.

Understanding the Science Behind Fermentation and Pickling

Fermentation and pickling are culinary arts deeply rooted in science. To master these techniques and create delicious preserved foods, it's essential to grasp the scientific principles at play. This section will delve into the intricate world of fermentation and pickling, exploring the science behind these time-honored processes.

At the heart of both fermentation and pickling is the microbial world. These techniques harness the power of microorganisms, mainly bacteria and yeasts, to transform the raw ingredients into flavorful and preserved delicacies. The key players in fermentation are lactic acid bacteria, while yeasts are pivotal in processes like bread baking and alcoholic fermentation. In pickling, lactic acid bacteria drive the acidification process, which convert sugars into lactic acid. This drop in pH creates an acidic environment that hinders the growth of harmful bacteria and preserves the food.

Temperature is crucial role in the success of fermentation. Different strains of microorganisms thrive at specific temperature ranges. For example, lactic acid bacteria prefer temperatures between 60-75°F (15-24°C), making them suitable for room temperature fermentation. Controlling the temperature ensures that the right microbes dominate fermentation, leading to desirable flavors and textures. Cooler temperatures slow fermentation, while warmer temperatures can accelerate it, so precise temperature management is essential.

Salt is a common ingredient in both fermentation and pickling, and its role is multifaceted. In fermentation, salt helps regulate microbial growth. It can inhibit the growth of undesirable bacteria while allowing lactic acid bacteria to flourish. Salt is used primarily in pickling for its preservation properties, helping to draw moisture out of vegetables through osmosis, creating a brine that preserves the ingredients. The salt concentration in the brine is crucial; too little can lead to spoilage, while too much can hinder fermentation. Achieving the right balance is key.

Water is the medium through which the magic of fermentation and pickling occurs. In both processes, water is essential to dissolve salt and sugar, creating the brine that envelops the ingredients. It is also the vehicle for the movement of nutrients, enzymes, and microorganisms within the fermenting or pickling vessel. Water quality is crucial, as chlorine or other contaminants can disrupt the microbial activity. Many fermentation enthusiasts opt for non-chlorinated water; some even use well or spring water to ensure purity.

The concept of anaerobic vs. aerobic fermentation is another scientific aspect to consider. Lactic acid bacteria can proliferate in anaerobic fermentation because it occurs in an oxygen-free environment. This type of fermentation is typical in processes like sauerkraut and kimchi. In contrast, aerobic fermentation involves exposure to oxygen and is commonly seen in alcoholic fermentation, such as beer and wine production. Understanding which type of fermentation your recipe requires is essential to achieving the desired results.

The role of enzymes in fermentation and pickling cannot be underestimated. Biological catalysts called enzymes let chemical processes happen more easily by disassembling complicated molecules into simpler ones. During fermentation, enzymes in the raw ingredients play a vital role in converting starches into sugars, which microorganisms can then ferment. In pickling, enzymes help soften the texture of vegetables over time, resulting in the desired pickled crunch. For instance, cucumbers contain an enzyme called pectinase, which softens the cucumbers' cell walls over time, leading to a crisp yet tender texture.

Time is a fundamental aspect of fermentation and pickling, intrinsically linked to the scientific processes at play. The fermentation or pickling duration directly affects the final product's flavor, texture, and safety.

Fermentation time determines the level of acidity and the development of complex flavors. Longer fermentation periods often yield more intense and tangy flavors. In pickling, the duration in the brine influences the degree of softening and preservation. Therefore, understanding the optimal time for each process is essential to achieving the desired results.

Acidity is a critical outcome of fermentation and pickling, driven by converting sugars into organic acids. In fermentation, lactic acid is the primary acid produced, contributing to the tangy flavor of fermented foods. The acidification process enhances flavor and acts as a natural preservative, creating an inhospitable environment for harmful bacteria. In pickling, acetic acid, a product of the fermentation of vinegar, is the primary acid responsible for preservation and flavor.

Microbial diversity is another fascinating aspect of fermentation and pickling. Different strains of bacteria and yeasts are present in various environments, contributing to the unique characteristics of fermented and pickled foods. The microbial community in sauerkraut differs from that in yogurt, resulting in distinct flavors and textures. Understanding and manipulating these microbial populations can lead to innovative and exciting culinary creations.

In conclusion, the science behind fermentation and pickling is a complex and fascinating world that underpins the art of food preservation. Microorganisms, temperature, salt, water, enzymes, time, and acidity are all critical factors that come into play during these processes. Mastery of these scientific principles allows us to unlock the full potential of fermentation and pickling, transforming ordinary ingredients into extraordinary preserved foods that delight the palate and nourish the body. By embracing the science behind these age-old techniques, we can continue to innovate and explore the boundless possibilities of culinary creativity.

CHAPTER II

Fermentation Basics

What Is Fermentation?

Fermentation is a remarkable and ancient biological process that has shaped the course of human civilization for thousands of years. It's a phenomenon that occurs in nature and is harnessed by humans to transform raw ingredients into various foods as well as beverages. At its core, fermentation is known as a metabolic process that includes the conversion of organic compounds, typically sugars and carbohydrates, into other compounds, such as alcohol or organic acids, by microorganisms, such as bacteria, yeasts, or molds. This transformative process has profound implications for both the preservation and enhancement of food, as well as the creation of unique and complex flavors.

One of the most iconic and widely recognized forms of fermentation is alcoholic fermentation, which is responsible for producing alcoholic beverages like beer, wine, and spirits. In this process, yeast, a microorganism, consumes sugars and converts them into alcohol and also carbon dioxide through a series of chemical reactions. The yeast's ability to perform this conversion makes beer bubbly and wine intoxicating. Alcoholic fermentation has been a part of human culture for millennia, with evidence of beer production dating back to ancient Mesopotamia around 3400 BCE.

However, fermentation extends far beyond the world of alcoholic beverages. Lactic acid fermentation is another common form that is pivotal in creating many fermented foods. Lactic acid bacteria, including Lactobacillus and Leuconostoc species, are the heroes of this type of fermentation. They consume sugars and produce lactic acid as a byproduct, leading to a drop in pH. This pH decrease preserves foods and gives them their characteristic tangy flavor. Iconic examples of lactic acid fermentation include yogurt, sauerkraut, kimchi, and various types of pickles.

Fermentation is critical in the world of breadmaking. Yeasts, whether naturally occurring in the environment or added as commercial starters, ferment the sugars in the dough, producing carbon dioxide gas. This gas becomes trapped in the dough, causing it to rise and expand. The result is the light and airy texture of bread that we all enjoy. Without fermentation, bread would be dense and heavy, lacking the delightful combination of a crispy crust and a soft interior.

Beyond beverages, dairy products, and bread, fermentation touches nearly every corner of the culinary world. Cheese is a prime example of how fermentation can transform milk into various textures and flavors. Different strains of bacteria and molds contribute to the unique characteristics of each cheese variety, from the creamy and mild Brie to the pungent and crumbly blue cheese.

Similarly, fermented condiments like soy sauce, miso, and fish sauce are staples in many cuisines, adding depth and complexity to dishes. These condiments are the result of fermentation processes that can take months or even years to complete. The microorganisms responsible for these transformations break down proteins and complex carbohydrates, yielding the savory and umami-rich flavors that enhance food taste.

In the realm of vegetables, fermentation has been a crucial technique for preserving seasonal harvests and providing essential nutrients during lean times.

Sauerkraut, for instance, is a classic fermented cabbage dish that originated in Eastern Europe. Cabbage is transformed into a tangy and crunchy condiment that can be enjoyed year-round through lactic acid fermentation. A staple in Korean cuisine, known as kimchi is another example of fermented vegetables, often made with a mix of cabbage, radishes, and various spices.

The benefits of fermentation extend beyond preservation and flavor enhancement; they also have nutritional advantages. Fermented foods are commonly rich in probiotics, which are beneficial microorganisms that can take part to a healthy gut microbiome. These probiotics may aid digestion, support the immune system, and promote mental well-being. Yogurt, kefir, and kombucha are well-known examples of probiotic-rich foods that have gained popularity for their potential health benefits.

Moreover, fermentation can increase the bioavailability of certain nutrients. For example, the fermentation of soybeans in producing soy sauce and miso can enhance the absorption of essential minerals and amino acids. This improved bioavailability can make fermented foods delicious and more nutritious.

The art of fermentation is deeply intertwined with culture and tradition. Different regions of the world have developed their unique fermented foods and beverages, reflecting their environmental conditions, available ingredients, and culinary preferences. For instance, the Japanese have mastered the art of sake production, while the Koreans have perfected kimchi recipes passed down through generations. These fermented delicacies provide sustenance and serve as cultural touchstones, connecting people to their heritage and the wisdom of their ancestors.

In conclusion, fermentation is a fascinating and diverse biological process that has shaped our culinary world and our connection to food. Whether it's the enthusiasm of a glass of champagne, the tang of sauerkraut, or the comforting aroma of freshly baked bread, fermentation is all around us. Its ability to convert humble ingredients into extraordinary flavors and its role in preservation and nutrition make it an indispensable part of human culture. As we continue to explore the science and art of fermentation, we unlock new possibilities for creativity, sustainability, and nourishment, reminding us that the power of microorganisms can yield some of the most profound and delicious experiences in the world of food.

Lactic Acid Fermentation

Lactic acid fermentation is a remarkable and time-honored biological process that humans have harnessed for centuries to preserve and transform food. This type of fermentation, driven by lactic acid bacteria, is responsible for the creation of some of our most beloved and iconic foods, from yogurt and sauerkraut to kimchi and sourdough bread. At its core, lactic acid fermentation is a metabolic pathway that converts sugars and carbohydrates into lactic acid, leading to a pH drop. This decrease in pH not only preserves food but also imparts the characteristic tangy flavor and desirable texture that make these fermented delicacies so irresistible.

The process of lactic acid fermentation begins with selecting raw ingredients rich in carbohydrates, such as vegetables, grains, or milk. These carbohydrates are the primary energy source for the lactic acid bacteria involved. In the case of dairy, lactose (milk sugar) is the carbohydrate of choice. In vegetables, the naturally occurring sugars like glucose and fructose provide the fuel for fermentation. When these ingredients are exposed to lactic acid bacteria, the transformation begins.

One of the most well-known examples of lactic acid fermentation is yogurt production. To make yogurt, milk is heated to kill off any competing microorganisms and is then cooled to a temperature suitable for the lactic acid bacteria to thrive. A small amount of yogurt culture is added to the milk, typically containing strains of Lactobacillus bulgaricus and Streptococcus thermophilus. These bacteria start consuming the lactose in the milk, breaking it down into glucose and galactose. This metabolic process produces lactic acid as a byproduct, leading to the characteristic tangy flavor of yogurt.

As lactic acid builds up in the milk, the pH decreases and an acidic environment is created. Because of the acidic environment, pathogenic bacteria cannot develop, ensuring the yogurt's safety and shelf life. Simultaneously, the proteins in the milk denature and coagulate under the acidic conditions, giving yogurt its creamy and thick texture.

Sauerkraut is another classic example of lactic acid fermentation, highlighting the versatility of this process. To make sauerkraut, cabbage is thinly sliced, salted, and then packed into a fermentation vessel. Initially, the brine is created when the salt uses osmosis to extract moisture from the cabbage. In this briny, anaerobic setting, lactic acid bacteria that are either naturally occurring on the cabbage or added through a starting culture start to flourish. As the bacteria consume the cabbage's sugars, they produce lactic acid, leading to the drop in pH that preserves the sauerkraut and imparts its tangy flavor.

The transformative power of lactic acid fermentation is not limited to vegetables and dairy. Grains can also undergo this process, resulting in sourdough bread, a culinary favorite known for its complex flavors and chewy texture. In sourdough breadmaking, wild yeast and lactic acid bacteria are harnessed from the environment or introduced through a sourdough starter culture. These microorganisms break down the flour's carbohydrates and release carbon dioxide and lactic acid as byproducts. The dough rises as a result of the trapped carbon dioxide gas, giving the bread its recognizable air pockets. The lactic acid contributes to the tangy flavor that distinguishes sourdough from conventional bread.

Lactic acid fermentation not only preserves and enhances food flavor but also offers significant nutritional benefits. Fermented foods such as yogurt as well as sauerkraut are rich in probiotics, beneficial microorganisms that can support a healthy gut microbiome. These probiotics may aid digestion, strengthen the immune system, and contribute to mental well-being. Consuming probiotic-rich foods has gained popularity for their potential health benefits, making them a staple in many diets worldwide.

Furthermore, lactic acid fermentation can increase the bioavailability of certain nutrients. For example, it can break down compounds called phytates present in grains, which can inhibit the absorption of crucial minerals like iron and zinc. This enhanced bioavailability can make fermented foods delicious and more nutritious.

The art of lactic acid fermentation is deeply intertwined with culture and tradition. Different regions of the world have developed their unique fermented foods, reflecting their available ingredients, environmental conditions, and culinary preferences. Kimchi, a spicy and pungent fermented vegetable dish, is a beloved staple in Korean cuisine. Its variations incorporate ingredients like cabbage, radishes, and a medley of spices, showcasing the diversity of flavors that can emerge from lactic acid fermentation.

In Eastern Europe, sauerkraut is a classic accompaniment to many dishes, while kefir, a fermented milk beverage, holds a special place in the culinary heritage of the Caucasus region. Each of these fermented creations reflects the cultural significance of food preservation and the appreciation for the complex and nuanced flavors that arise from this ancient process.

The science of lactic acid fermentation continues to evolve, as researchers explore new strains of lactic acid bacteria and their potential applications. This ongoing exploration has led to traditional and contemporary fermentation practices innovations. Whether it's experimenting with different vegetable combinations, refining fermentation techniques, or exploring novel applications in the culinary world, lactic acid fermentation remains a dynamic and ever-relevant process.

In conclusion, lactic acid fermentation is a captivating and versatile biological process that has left an indelible mark on our culinary traditions and our appreciation for flavor. From the creamy goodness of yogurt to the crunchy tang of sauerkraut and the complex allure of sourdough bread, lactic acid fermentation has enriched our palates and nourished our bodies for generations. Its ability to convert humble ingredients into extraordinary culinary delights and its potential health benefits continue to make it a cherished and revered aspect of our culinary heritage. As we celebrate the magic of lactic acid fermentation, we honor the ancient wisdom that reminds us of the power of microorganisms to create some of the most extraordinary and delicious experiences in the world of food.

Wild vs. Commercial Starter Cultures

Fermentation, the transformative process that turns raw ingredients into a world of flavorful delicacies, owes its magic to microorganisms. These tiny beings, often invisible to the naked eye, wield immense power in the culinary world. Among the most critical players in fermentation are starter cultures, which consist of specific strains of microorganisms carefully selected to kickstart and guide the fermentation process. Two primary categories of starter cultures exist: wild cultures, hailing from the environment, and commercial cultures, cultivated under controlled conditions. Understanding the differences and advantages of each is essential for mastering the art of fermentation.

Wild cultures, as the name suggests, originate from the environment and are often naturally occurring on the surface of vegetables, fruits, grains, or even in the air. They encompass various microorganisms, including bacteria, yeasts, and molds, which can vary widely depending on the geographic location, climate, and specific environmental conditions. Wild cultures have been used for centuries, passed down through generations, and are integral to traditional and artisanal fermentation practices. They possess the charm of unpredictability, as the specific microorganisms present in a wild culture can vary from batch to batch, leading to unique and complex flavor profiles. Sauerkraut made with a wild culture from one region may taste subtly different from sauerkraut made in another, reflecting the local microbial terroir.

On the other hand, commercial starter cultures are precisely formulated and controlled mixtures of specific microorganisms. They are cultured, propagated, and packaged under controlled conditions in laboratories or production facilities. These cultures consist of well-characterized strains, often isolated from the wild, and are selected for their consistency, reliability, and ability to produce desired characteristics in the final product. Commercial starter cultures offer a level of predictability and consistency that can be crucial for large-scale food production and ensuring a uniform product quality. For example, the distinct flavor and texture of Swiss cheese or the consistent fizz of kombucha are achieved through the use of commercial starter cultures.

The choice between wild and commercial starter cultures depends on various factors, including the type of fermentation, the desired flavor and texture, and the production scale. Wild cultures thrive in small-scale, artisanal settings, emphasizing tradition, diversity, and the subtle nuances of flavor that arise from local microorganisms. These cultures are often used in traditional processes like sourdough breadmaking, where bakers cultivate the natural yeasts and lactic acid bacteria present in their environment to create distinctive bread.

On the other hand, commercial starter cultures are indispensable for large-scale food production, where consistency and efficiency are paramount. In the production of yogurt, for instance, specific strains of Lactobacillus bulgaricus as well as Streptococcus thermophilus are used to ensure a consistent texture and flavor in every batch. Similarly, the controlled fermentation of alcoholic beverages like beer or wine relies on carefully selected yeast strains to achieve predictable alcohol content and flavor profiles.

One significant advantage of wild cultures is their ability to create unique and complex flavors. The microbial diversity in a wild culture introduces a wide range of metabolites and compounds that add to the taste and aroma of the final product. For example, the natural microorganisms present in sourdough starter cultures can produce a complex bouquet of flavors, including tangy acidity, nutty undertones, and hints of fruitiness, making each loaf a sensory adventure. In the world of cheese, artisanal producers may rely on wild cultures to develop their signature flavor profiles, resulting in cheeses with regional character and distinct terroirs.

However, the diversity of wild cultures can also be a double-edged sword. While it can lead to unique flavors, it can also introduce unpredictability and challenges in consistency and control. The variability in microbial composition from batch to batch can make it challenging to precisely replicate a particular flavor profile. Moreover, there is always the risk of contamination by undesirable microorganisms, which can lead to spoilage or off-flavors.

Commercial starter cultures offer a solution to these challenges with their standardized and well-characterized strains. They provide a level of control and predictability that is essential for large-scale production and quality assurance. For example, commercial starter cultures in dairy fermentation allow manufacturers to produce consistent and safe products with precisely defined flavor profiles. This level of control ensures that consumers can enjoy the same taste and texture of yogurt or cheese every time they purchase their favorite brand.

While commercial starter cultures excel in consistency and predictability, they may lack the depth and complexity of flavors associated with wild cultures. The narrow selection of microorganisms in commercial cultures may result in a more uniform but less intricate taste profile. Some artisanal producers argue that using commercial cultures can lead to a loss of regional and traditional flavors, as standardized strains replace the unique microbial populations of a specific area.

There has been a growing interest in bridging the gap between wild and commercial cultures through a hybrid approach in recent years. Some producers are exploring ways to capture the essence of wild fermentation while maintaining control and consistency. They do so by using commercial starter cultures as a foundation and allowing for the incorporation of wild microorganisms from the environment. This approach aims to balance the reliability of commercial cultures and the complexity of flavors associated with wild fermentation.

In conclusion, the choice between wild and commercial starter cultures in fermentation is a decision that depends on a range of factors, including the desired outcome, scale of production, and the values of tradition and consistency. Both approaches have their merits, offering unique advantages and challenges. Wild cultures celebrate the diversity and complexity of flavors, while commercial cultures ensure consistency and control. As fermentation continues to evolve as both a culinary art and a science, producers and enthusiasts are finding ways to harness the best of both worlds, preserving tradition while embracing innovation and creativity. Ultimately, whether you opt for wild or commercial starter cultures, the world of fermentation remains a captivating journey into the transformative power of microorganisms and the flavors they unlock.

The Fermentation Process Step by Step

The fermentation process is a captivating journey into the realm of culinary alchemy, where the transformation of raw ingredients unfolds through the actions of microorganisms. This age-old technique has been practiced by civilizations for thousands of years, yielding a vast array of foods and beverages that are both delicious and preserved. To understand and master the art of fermentation, it's essential to delve into the intricate steps that microorganisms follow, guided by the careful orchestration of factors like temperature, time, and ingredient selection. In this section, we will explore the fermentation process step-by-step, revealing the magic that occurs at each stage.

Step 1: Ingredient Selection The journey begins with carefully selecting ingredients rich in carbohydrates, such as fruits, vegetables, grains, or milk. These carbohydrates serve as the primary energy source for the microorganisms involved in fermentation. The choice of ingredients depends on the desired end product. For example, grapes are selected for winemaking, milk for cheese production, and cabbage for sauerkraut. The chosen ingredients' quality, freshness, and ripeness are significant in the success of fermentation, as they directly influence the final product's flavor, texture, and nutritional value.

Step 2: Preparation Once the ingredients are selected, they undergo preparation to create an environment conducive to fermentation. This preparation can vary widely depending on the type of fermentation and the desired outcome. For vegetables like cabbage in sauerkraut making, preparation may involve shredding, salting, and massaging to draw out moisture and create a brine. In dairy fermentation, milk may be heated and cooled to specific temperatures to activate enzymes or pasteurize it, eliminating competing microorganisms. Grains may be milled or crushed to expose starches and increase their surface area for microbial activity.

Step 3: Inoculation Inoculation is the introduction of microorganisms into the prepared ingredients to initiate fermentation. Microorganisms can come from various sources, including naturally occurring populations on the ingredients themselves, the environment, or a carefully selected starter culture. A starter culture consists of specific strains of microorganisms chosen for their ability to produce the desired flavor, texture, and safety profile. For example, yogurt is inoculated with Lactobacillus bulgaricus and Streptococcus thermophilus strains, while sourdough bread relies on naturally occurring wild yeast and lactic acid bacteria.

Step 4: Fermentation Fermentation is the heart of the process, where microorganisms work their magic on the ingredients. During fermentation, microorganisms metabolize the carbohydrates present in the ingredients, converting them into various compounds, such as organic acids, alcohol, and carbon dioxide. These metabolic activities result in the final product's characteristic flavors, textures, and preservation. The length of fermentation varies based on the type of fermentation and the desired outcome. It can range from hours to weeks or even months. For example, yogurt may ferment for several hours, while sauerkraut can take weeks to develop its tangy flavor fully.

Step 5: pH and Acidity Regulation One crucial aspect of fermentation is the regulation of pH and acidity. As microorganisms metabolize carbohydrates, they produce organic acids, such as lactic acid or acetic acid. These acids lower the pH of the fermenting medium, creating an acidic environment. The drop in pH serves several purposes. It preserves the final product by inhibiting the growth of harmful bacteria. It also contributes to the tangy flavor characteristic of many fermented foods. The control of pH and acidity is crucial for guaranteeing the safety and quality of the finished product.

Step 6: Flavor Development Flavor development is a dynamic and intricate aspect of fermentation. During this stage, the interaction between microorganisms and the ingredients results in the creation of complex flavor compounds. These compounds include esters, aldehydes, and volatile organic compounds that contribute to the unique aroma as well as taste of the final product. The diversity of microorganisms and the metabolic pathways they follow influence the flavor profile. For instance, the yeast and lactic acid bacteria strains in a sourdough starter culture produce a wide range of compounds responsible for its distinct tangy and nutty flavor.

Step 7: Texture and Consistency Texture and consistency are equally important factors in fermentation. Microorganisms can impact the texture of the final product by various means. For example, lactic acid bacteria in yogurt produce exopolysaccharides that contribute to its creamy and smooth texture. In the case of bread, the carbon dioxide gas produced by yeast fermentation causes the dough to rise, creating the airy and light texture of bread. The control of temperature, time, and fermentation conditions is essential for achieving the desired texture as well as consistency.

Step 8: Maturation and Aging After the primary fermentation, many fermented products undergo maturation or aging. The flavors continue to develop and mature during this period, often becoming more complex and nuanced. Cheese wheels, for example, may be aged for months or even years, with different stages of aging resulting in distinct flavor profiles. Similarly, wines and spirits may be aged in wooden barrels to impart additional flavors and characteristics to the beverage.

Step 9: Preservation One of the primary reasons for fermenting foods is preservation. The acidic environment made by the fermentation process inhibits the growth of harmful molds, bacteria, and yeasts, extending the final product's shelf life. Fermented foods can be stored for extended periods without the need for refrigeration or artificial preservatives. This preservation aspect has been crucial for communities throughout history, allowing them to store and consume seasonal harvests year-round.

Step 10: Enjoyment The final step in the fermentation process is enjoying the finished product. Fermented foods as well as beverages have played a vital role in culinary traditions worldwide, offering diverse flavors, textures, and nutritional benefits. From the crisp tang of sauerkraut to the creamy richness of yogurt, the world of fermentation invites us to savor the results of nature's transformative power.

In conclusion, the fermentation process is a captivating journey unfolding in meticulously orchestrated steps. From ingredient selection to inoculation, fermentation, and maturation, each stage contributes to creating flavors and textures that delight the palate and preserve nature's bounty. The careful management of factors like temperature, pH, and time ensures that fermentation results in safe and high-quality products. As we explore and appreciate the intricacies of fermentation, we celebrate the ancient wisdom that has allowed us to unlock the magic of microorganisms and their transformative power in the world of culinary arts.

CHAPTER III

Pickling Fundamentals

Introduction to Pickling

Pickling is a fascinating and ancient method of preserving food, extending the shelf life of perishable items and enhancing their flavors and nutritional value. This section delves into the historical background, techniques, types, benefits, and cultural significance of pickling, providing a comprehensive overview of this enduring culinary practice.

The history of pickling dates back thousands of years, with evidence suggesting that the ancient Mesopotamians may have been the first to pickle foods around 2400 B.C. The primary purpose of pickling at that time, as it is today, was to preserve food for longer periods, especially to sustain through seasons when fresh food was scarce. This method of preservation was vital for survival, particularly for sailors and travelers who needed to store food for long voyages. Over time, pickling spread across the globe, with each culture developing its unique methods and flavors, from the spicy kimchi of Korea to the tangy sauerkraut of Germany.

Pickling is essentially the process of preserving food by anaerobic fermentation in brine or vinegar. The high acidity of the pickling solution kills bacteria, preventing spoilage and allowing the food to be stored for an extended period. There are two primary methods of pickling: fermentation pickling and vinegar pickling. Fermentation pickling involves submerging the food in a brine solution, creating an environment where beneficial bacteria (mainly Lactobacillus) can thrive and ferment the food, producing lactic acid. This not only preserves the food but also can improve gut health due to the probiotics created during the fermentation process. On the other hand, vinegar pickling uses vinegar mixed with water, and often sugar and spices, to create an acidic solution that pickles the food without fermentation.

Each method of pickling offers a variety of flavors and textures, depending on the ingredients and techniques used. For instance, cucumbers can be pickled to create the classic dill pickle, while beets, onions, carrots, and even fruits like apples as well as pears can also be preserved through pickling. The choice of spices and herbs added to the pickling solution further customizes the flavor, allowing for endless variations ranging from sweet and mild to spicy and tangy.

The benefits of pickling extend beyond flavor enhancement and food preservation. Pickled foods are rich in vitamins and antioxidants, boosting the immune system as well as enhancing overall health. Fermented pickles are particularly beneficial as they contain live cultures that is similar to those found in yogurt, which enhance a healthy digestive system. Moreover, pickling can be a sustainable way to reduce food waste by preserving seasonal produce that might otherwise spoil.

Culturally, pickling holds significant importance in many societies worldwide, often associated with traditional celebrations and family gatherings. In Eastern Europe, pickled cucumbers and sauerkraut are staples, while in Asia, varieties of pickled vegetables and kimchi are essential to the cuisine. These traditions not only preserve the food but also cultural heritage, passing down recipes and techniques from generation to generation.

Despite its ancient origins, pickling remains highly relevant in modern cuisine, both for its practical benefits and its ability to add depth as well as complexity to dishes. Chefs and home cooks alike experiment with pickling to create unique flavors and textures, incorporating pickled ingredients into everything from salads and sandwiches to cocktails and desserts.

However, it's important to note that while pickling can enhance the nutritional value of food, it also increases sodium content, which can be a concern for individuals with certain health conditions. Therefore, it's advisable to consume pickled foods in moderation as part of a balanced diet.

In conclusion, pickling is a remarkable culinary technique that bridges the past and the present, offering a sustainable method to preserve food, enrich flavors, and maintain nutritional value. Its versatility and health benefits have made it a beloved practice worldwide, transcending cultures and generations. Whether through the tangy crunch of a dill pickle or the complex flavors of kimchi, pickling continues to be celebrated for its ability to transform simple ingredients into something extraordinary, proving that this ancient practice is more than just a method of preservation—it's an art form that enriches our culinary heritage and daily lives.

The Role of Vinegar

The role of vinegar in pickling is both central and multifaceted, serving as a cornerstone of this ancient preservation technique that spans cultures and millennia. This section explores the significance of vinegar in pickling, from its preservation capabilities to its impact on flavor, health benefits, and the cultural traditions it upholds. Understanding the role of vinegar provides insight into the science and art of pickling, illustrating why this method remains prevalent in culinary practices around the world.

Vinegar, a versatile and ancient ingredient, has been used in culinary applications for thousands of years, with its origins traced back to civilizations such as the Babylonians and the ancient Chinese. It is generated through the fermentation of ethanol by acetic acid bacteria, which converts alcohol into acetic acid, giving vinegar its distinctive sour taste and potent antimicrobial properties. These properties make vinegar an ideal agent for pickling, a process where food items are preserved in an acidic environment.

The preservation power of vinegar lies in its high acidity, which creates an inhospitable environment for harmful bacteria and enzymes that cause food spoilage. When vegetables, fruits, or even meats are submerged in a vinegar solution, the acidic medium effectively halts microbial growth, ensuring the food remains safe and edible for extended periods. This has been a crucial technique for human survival, particularly before the advent of modern refrigeration, allowing people to store food through harsh winters or long journeys.

Beyond preservation, vinegar profoundly influences the flavor profile of pickled products. It imparts a tangy, sharp taste that can be balanced with the addition of salts, sugars, and a variety of spices and herbs. The type of vinegar used—be it white vinegar, apple cider vinegar, rice vinegar, or others—further diversifies the flavors of pickled items, allowing for a wide range of culinary applications. This versatility is what makes vinegar-based pickling a popular technique not just for preserving food but also for enhancing its taste and texture.

In addition to its preservative and flavor-enhancing qualities, vinegar-based pickling offers numerous health benefits. Vinegar itself is known for its health-promoting properties, including blood sugar control, weight management, and antimicrobial effects. When used in pickling, it can help retain or even amplify the nutritional content of the pickled items, such as vitamins, antioxidants, and minerals. Furthermore, though vinegar-pickled foods do not contain the live probiotics found in fermented pickles, they still contribute to a balanced diet by providing an additional source of enzymes and beneficial acids.

Culturally, vinegar has played a significant role in the pickling traditions of many societies. In Eastern Europe, vinegar is a key ingredient in the preparation of pickled cucumbers, beets, and cabbages, essential to the regional cuisine. Asian countries utilize rice vinegar and other types to pickle a variety of vegetables and fruits, creating dishes that are integral to their culinary heritage. In the Americas, vinegar-based pickles accompany meals as both a flavor enhancer as well as a digestive aid. These traditions highlight the importance of vinegar in connecting people to their cultural heritage through food.

Despite its many advantages, the use of vinegar in pickling must be approached with care, particularly regarding concentration and quality. The acidity level, typically measured as pH, needs to be sufficiently high (low pH value) to ensure safety and preservation. Moreover, the choice of vinegar can affect the overall taste and quality of the pickled product, with each type providing a unique flavor profile and potential health benefits. This necessitates a thoughtful selection of vinegar based on the desired outcome, whether it be for flavor, health, or preservation purposes.

Today, the art and science of vinegar-based pickling continue to evolve, with chefs and home cooks experimenting with different types of vinegar and pickling techniques to create innovative dishes. This experimentation not only leads to new culinary creations but also reinforces the role of vinegar as a pivotal ingredient in the global food landscape. Furthermore, the growing interest in DIY and sustainable living practices has spurred a resurgence in home pickling, highlighting vinegar's enduring relevance in food preservation.

In conclusion, vinegar's role in pickling is indispensable, offering a blend of preservation, flavor enhancement, health benefits, and cultural significance. Its acidic nature is fundamental to the pickling process, enabling the safe storage of foods while imbuing them with distinct tastes and textures. The variety of vinegars available allows for a broad spectrum of pickled products, each with its unique characteristics and culinary applications. Moreover, the health attributes of vinegar, combined with the nutritional preservation of pickling, contribute positively to dietary practices. As a bearer of tradition, vinegar helps maintain the cultural identity of cuisines across the globe, preserving not just food but the heritage and memories associated with it. Thus, the role of vinegar in pickling transcends mere preservation, embodying the essence of culinary artistry and cultural continuity.

Types of Pickles

The world of pickles is vast and varied, encompassing a wide range of flavors, textures, and ingredients that reflect the diverse culinary traditions of the globe. Pickles are more than just a tangy accompaniment to meals; they are a testament to the ingenuity of human culinary practices, offering a window into the cultural heritage of different societies. This section delves into the myriad types of pickles, exploring their unique characteristics, preparation methods, and the cultural significance they hold.

At the heart of pickling lies the basic principle of preservation, a technique that has been refined across centuries and civilizations. Through the use of vinegar, salt, and fermentation, foods that would otherwise perish quickly are transformed into enduring delicacies. The process not only extends the shelf life of the produce but also enhances its flavors, resulting in a product that is often more vibrant and complex than its fresh counterpart.

One of the most common and beloved types of pickles are cucumber pickles, which are ubiquitous in many parts of the world. These can range from the crisp and tart dill pickles familiar in American cuisine to the sweet, spiced gherkins found in European pantries. The versatility of cucumber pickles is evident in their varying degrees of sourness, sweetness, and spice, which are achieved through different pickling solutions and techniques.

Another popular category is the fermented vegetable pickles, such as sauerkraut and kimchi. Sauerkraut, with its origins in German cuisine, is made from fermented cabbage and is renowned for its sour, tangy flavor that complements a variety of dishes, from sausages to stews. Kimchi, a staple in Korean cuisine, takes the concept of fermented cabbage to a new level with the addition of a rich blend of spices, garlic, and chili peppers, resulting in a pickle that is both spicy and deeply flavorful. These fermented pickles are not only cherished for their taste but also for their health benefits, as the fermentation process promotes the growth of probiotics beneficial to the digestive system.

Fruit pickles are another delightful variety, showcasing the creative use of sweet, tart, and spicy flavors. In many South Asian countries, mango pickles are a cherished condiment, made by pickling unripe mangoes in a mixture of oil, spices, as well as salt. The result is a pickle that is intensely flavorful, with a perfect balance of sour, sweet, and spicy notes. Similarly, pickled lemons and limes add a vibrant citrusy zing to dishes in Middle Eastern and North African cuisines, illustrating the global love for pickled fruits.

In addition to these, there are countless other types of pickles made from a wide array of vegetables and even meats. For instance, pickled onions are a common sight in British pubs, often served alongside cheeses and cold cuts. Japanese cuisine features tsukemono, a variety of pickles made from vegetables like radishes, cucumbers, and eggplants, each with its special flavor profile ranging from sweet to umami. Meanwhile, in parts of Eastern Europe and Asia, pickled fish and meats are traditional delicacies, preserved through salting and fermentation to extend their shelf life and enhance their taste.

The preparation methods of pickles vary as widely as the types themselves. While some pickles are made through quick pickling, a process that involves marinating the produce in a vinegar-based brine for a short period, others require fermentation, where the natural sugars in the vegetables are transformed into lactic acid by beneficial bacteria over several weeks or even months. Each method distributes unique flavors and textures to the pickles, from the crisp, vinegary bite of quick pickles to the complex, tangy depth of fermented ones.

Cultural significance is deeply intertwined with the practice of pickling, with many types of pickles being integral to the identity of the cuisines they belong to. For example, the making and sharing of kimchi are central to Korean culture, symbolizing the importance of community and tradition. In India, the preparation of pickles is a time-honored ritual, with recipes and techniques passed down through generations, making each family's pickle recipe a cherished heirloom.

In conclusion, the world of pickles is a rich tapestry of flavors, textures, and traditions, reflecting the diversity and creativity of culinary practices around the globe. From the crunchy dill pickles of American barbecues to the fiery kimchi of Korean feasts, pickles add depth and excitement to meals, transcending their role as mere side dishes to become cultural icons in their own right. The types of pickles discussed in this section are but a glimpse into the vast array of pickled delicacies available, each with its unique story and place in the culinary world. As we explore and savor these varied types of pickles, we not only indulge in their delightful flavors but also connect with the rich cultural histories and traditions that they represent.

Quick Pickling vs. Fermented Pickling

Pickling, a method treasured across cultures for preserving food, comes in various forms, each with unique characteristics and outcomes. Among these, quick pickling and fermented pickling stand out for their distinct processes and the flavors they impart to the produce. This section explores the nuances of quick pickling versus fermented pickling, delving into their methods, benefits, flavors, and uses in culinary practices, providing a comprehensive understanding of these preservation techniques.

Quick pickling, as the name suggests, is a swift process that involves immersing fruits, vegetables, or even meats in a vinegar-based brine. This method is designed for immediate consumption or short-term storage, making it a popular choice for home cooks and professional chefs alike. The brine, typically a mixture of vinegar, water, salt, and sugar, is boiled and then poured over the produce, which has been prepared and placed in jars. The high acidity of the vinegar acts as a preservative, hindering the growth of harmful bacteria and extending the shelf life of the food. Spices and herbs are often added to the brine, infusing the pickles with complex flavors that is ranging from sweet and tangy to spicy and aromatic. Quick pickles can be ready to eat within hours or days, offering a crunchy, flavorful addition to meals with minimal effort.

Fermented pickling, on the other hand, is a time-honored technique that relies on the natural fermentation process to preserve and flavor the food. This method involves submerging the produce in a saltwater brine, creating an anaerobic environment conducive to the growth of beneficial bacteria, primarily Lactobacillus. Lactic acid, a naturally occurring preservative, is produced by these bacteria when they feed on the natural sugars in food. The fermentation process can take anywhere from a few days to several months, depending on the desired level of sourness and the specific recipe being used. Fermented pickles are characterized by their complex, tangy flavor and potential health benefits, as the fermentation process promotes the growth of probiotics, beneficial for gut health.

The differences between quick pickling and fermented pickling extend beyond their preparation methods to include their flavor profiles, health benefits, and culinary uses. Quick pickles tend to retain the fresh taste of the produce, complemented by the acidity of the vinegar and the added spices. This makes them an excellent choice for adding a crisp, acidic note to dishes, enhancing the overall flavor without overwhelming it. Quick pickles are often used as condiments, side dishes, or garnishes, providing a refreshing contrast to rich, savory meals.

Fermented pickles, in contrast, offer a depth of flavor that is both rich and complex, with a pronounced tanginess that develops over time. The slow fermentation process allows the flavors to meld and evolve, resulting in pickles that are both savory and sour, with a hint of umami. These pickles are not only valued for their taste but also for their nutritional benefits, as the probiotics produced during fermentation can aid digestion and support a healthy microbiome. Fermented pickles are versatile in their use, serving as a standalone snack, a flavorful addition to salads and sandwiches, or a traditional accompaniment to meals in various cultures.

The choice between quick pickling and fermented pickling often depends on personal preference, the desired outcome, and the time available. Quick pickling is ideal for those seeking immediate results and a straightforward preservation method that highlights the freshness of the produce. It is also well-suited for preserving a wide variety of foods, from classic cucumbers and carrots to more unconventional choices like watermelon rinds and grapes. Fermented pickling, while requiring more patience, rewards the effort with its distinctive flavors and health benefits. It appeals to those interested in traditional preservation methods and the cultivation of probiotic-rich foods.

In addition to their culinary applications, both quick pickling and fermented pickling reflect a growing interest in sustainable living and food preservation. These techniques increase the shelf life of seasonal vegetables, which helps to decrease food waste. They also connect us to cultural traditions, as pickling has been a part of human culinary practices for millennia, serving as a link to our ancestors and their ingenious ways of making food last longer.

In conclusion, quick pickling and fermented pickling represent two sides of the same coin, each with its unique advantages, flavors, and uses. Quick pickling offers a fast, easy way to preserve and enjoy the bounty of the garden, while fermented pickling provides a deeper dive into the world of flavors and the health benefits of probiotic foods. Both methods enrich our culinary repertoire, allowing us to savor the art of preservation and the delicious results it yields. Whether one prefers the immediate satisfaction of quick pickles or the complex, developed flavors of fermented ones, pickling in any form is a celebration of food, tradition, and the timeless human endeavor to harness nature's abundance.

CHAPTER IV

Fermented Vegetables

Making Sauerkraut

Sauerkraut, a fermented cabbage dish, has been a staple in diets across many cultures, particularly in German, Eastern European, and Russian cuisines. Its origins can be traced back centuries, serving as both a method for preserving cabbage through the winter months and a source of vital nutrients during times when fresh vegetables were scarce. This section delves into the process of making sauerkraut, exploring its historical significance, the fermentation process, health benefits, and culinary uses, providing a comprehensive overview of this beloved fermented food.

The process of making sauerkraut begins with the simplest of ingredients: cabbage and salt. The traditional method involves thinly slicing the cabbage and then massaging it with salt. The salt serves several purposes; it draws out water from the cabbage, creating a brine in which the cabbage can ferment, inhibits the growth of harmful bacteria, and promotes the fermentation process by lactobacillus bacteria present on the cabbage leaves. These bacteria are beneficial and naturally occurring, transforming the sugars in the cabbage into a lactic acid, which acts as a natural preservative.

Historically, sauerkraut was made in large batches at the end of the harvest season. Families would gather to chop and salt the cabbage, then pack it tightly into large crocks or barrels. The packed cabbage would then be weighed down, often with a clean stone or a sealed bag of water, to keep the cabbage submerged in its brine. This anaerobic environment is crucial for the fermentation process, preventing the growth of mold and ensuring that the cabbage ferments properly. The crocks would be stored in a cool, dark place, such as a cellar, where the sauerkraut would ferment over several weeks or even months.

The fermentation process is both an art and a science, requiring patience and attention to detail. As the cabbage ferments, it undergoes significant changes, not only in flavor but also in texture and nutritional content. The lactic acid produced during fermentation gives sauerkraut its characteristic tangy flavor, while also preserving the cabbage and preventing spoilage. The fermentation process also expands the bioavailability of nutrients, making sauerkraut a rich source of vitamin C, dietary fiber, and probiotics, which are beneficial for gut health.

Sauerkraut's health benefits are manifold. The probiotics produced during fermentation can help to balance the gut microbiome, supporting digestion and the immune system. The high fiber content promotes digestive health, while vitamin C and antioxidants contribute to overall well-being. Moreover, sauerkraut is low in calories and high in calcium and magnesium, making it a nutritious addition to any diet.

Culinarily, sauerkraut is incredibly versatile. It can be enjoyed raw, which preserves its probiotic benefits, or cooked, which can mellow its flavor and make it a more palatable addition to a variety of dishes. Sauerkraut is traditionally served alongside dishes like pork, sausages, and potatoes, adding a burst of tangy flavor that complements rich, hearty meals. It can also be used as a topping for sandwiches and hot dogs, incorporated into salads, or even included in soups and stews.

Making sauerkraut at home is a simple and rewarding process. It requires minimal equipment and ingredients but yields a product that is superior in taste and nutritional value to most store-bought versions. The key to successful sauerkraut is ensuring that the cabbage remains submerged in its brine throughout the fermentation process, which may require checking on it periodically and skimming off any foam or mold that may form on the surface. The fermentation time can differ based on the temperature and the desired sourness of the sauerkraut; cooler temperatures slow the fermentation process, while warmer temperatures accelerate it.

In conclusion, making sauerkraut is a practice steeped in history, offering a connection to our culinary past and a way to preserve and enjoy the bounty of the harvest. The process of fermenting cabbage into sauerkraut transforms simple ingredients into a complex, flavorful, and nutritious food that has been cherished by generations. Its health benefits, particularly its probiotic properties, make it a valuable addition to the diet, supporting gut health and overall wellness. Moreover, sauerkraut's culinary versatility allows it to be incorporated into an array of dishes, from traditional to contemporary, enriching our meals with its distinctive tangy flavor. Whether enjoyed on its own or as part of a dish, sauerkraut exemplifies the beauty and benefits of fermented foods, a testament to the wisdom of traditional food preservation methods and their enduring relevance in our modern culinary landscape.

Fermented Pickles

Fermented pickles represent a culinary tradition that spans across cultures and epochs, embodying a symbiosis between human ingenuity and the natural process of fermentation. This method of food preservation, while simple in its essence, harnesses the transformative power of microorganisms to convert fresh produce into long-lasting, flavorful, and health-enhancing delicacies. This section delves into the art and science of fermented pickles, exploring their historical roots, the fermentation process, their health benefits, and their place in global cuisines.

The origins of fermented pickles are as old as agriculture itself, with evidence suggesting that the practice began over 4,000 years ago in ancient Mesopotamia. As humans began cultivating crops, they also discovered the need to preserve excess produce for leaner times. Fermentation emerged as a natural solution to this problem, with various cultures around the world developing their unique versions of fermented pickles. From the spicy kimchi of Korea to the sour dills of Eastern Europe, fermented pickles have been a staple in diets, celebrated not only for their ability to extend the shelf life of foods but also for their distinctive flavors and health benefits.

Fermentation is a metabolic process that occurs when natural bacteria feed on the sugars as well as starches in food, producing lactic acid. This process, known as lacto-fermentation, is what lies at the heart of making fermented pickles. Vegetables submerged in a brine solution (water mixed with salt) create an anaerobic (oxygen-free) environment that favors the growth of Lactobacillus bacteria. These bacteria are naturally present on the surface of all vegetables and, under the right conditions, proliferate, producing lactic acid which acts as a natural preservative. The lactic acid, impedes the growth of harmful bacteria and also imparts a tangy flavor to the pickles, making them a delicious addition to any meal.

The benefits of fermented pickles extend far beyond their taste and preservation qualities. These pickles are a rich source of probiotics, beneficial bacteria that is crucial in maintaining gut health. Having foods that are rich in probiotics, like fermented pickles, can help balance the gut microbiota, improving digestion and enhancing the immune system. Furthermore, the fermentation process can increase the bioavailability of nutrients, making certain vitamins and minerals more accessible to the body. Fermented pickles are also low in calories and can be a substantial source of K and C vitamins, along with minerals such as iron and potassium.

Fermented pickles are incredibly diverse, with almost any vegetable being a candidate for fermentation. While cucumbers are perhaps the most commonly fermented vegetable, other popular choices include carrots, radishes, cabbage, and green beans. Each type of vegetable brings its unique flavors and textures to the fermentation process, and by adding herbs, spices, or even fruits to the brine, artisans and home cooks alike can create an endless variety of pickled delights. This versatility allows fermented pickles to be incorporated into an array of dishes, from salads and sandwiches to main courses, providing a burst of flavor and a contrast in texture that can elevate any meal.

Despite their global popularity, making fermented pickles can be an intimidating process for the uninitiated. However, the basic principles of fermentation are straightforward and require minimal equipment. The key to successful fermentation is maintaining the right conditions for the Lactobacillus bacteria to thrive. This includes keeping the vegetables submerged in the brine to create an anaerobic environment, using the correct proportion of salt to water to prevent the growth of undesirable microorganisms, and storing the fermenting vegetables at a stable temperature. Additionally, patience is necessary because, depending on the temperature and desired level of sourness, the fermentation process can take a few days to several weeks.

The cultural significance of fermented pickles cannot be overstated. In many cultures, pickling traditions are passed down through generations, with recipes and techniques closely guarded as family treasures. Fermented pickles also play a role in seasonal and religious festivities, symbolizing both the preservation of food and the preservation of cultural identity. In recent years, there has been a resurgence of interest in fermented foods, driven by a growing awareness of their health benefits and a desire to reconnect with traditional food practices. This has led to a renaissance in artisanal pickling, with chefs and food enthusiasts experimenting with new flavor combinations and fermentation techniques.

In conclusion, fermented pickles are a testament to the enduring wisdom of traditional food preservation methods. They represent a perfect blend of flavor, nutrition, and sustainability, offering a practical solution to food preservation that also enriches our diets with probiotics and vital nutrients. The process of making fermented pickles, while rooted in ancient practices, continues to evolve, reflecting the creativity and diversity of global cuisines. As we rediscover the joys of fermentation, fermented pickles stand out as a delicious reminder of the connections between culture, health, and the simple pleasures of eating well.

Kimchi and Other Fermented Delights

Kimchi, the quintessential Korean fermented delicacy, stands as a testament to the ingenuity of traditional culinary practices that have spanned centuries. This spicy, tangy, and sometimes pungent side dish is more than just a staple in Korean cuisine; it is a cultural icon, embodying the flavors, history, and soul of Korea. However, kimchi is but one star in the vast universe of fermented delights that populate culinary traditions around the globe. These fermented foods, ranging from sauerkraut in Germany to miso in Japan, not only offer a unique window into the cultures that cherish them but also provide remarkable health benefits and contribute to the sustainability of food practices. This section explores the world of kimchi and other fermented delights, their cultural significance, health benefits, and the fermentation process that transforms simple ingredients into complex, flavorful, and nutritious foods.

Kimchi's origins can be traced back to ancient times, evolving from a simple method of preserving vegetables to a diverse array of fermented dishes that vary by region, season, and family tradition. The most common version, baechu kimchi, is made with napa cabbage, seasoned with a paste of chili peppers, garlic, ginger, and other different ingredients, including fish sauce or fermented shrimp. The mixture is then allowed to ferment for days, weeks, or even months, developing its characteristic depth of flavor. Kimchi is not only a side dish but also an ingredient in numerous Korean dishes, from stews and soups to pancakes and fried rice, showcasing its versatility and integral role in Korean cuisine.

Beyond kimchi, the world of fermented foods is rich and diverse. In Eastern Europe, sauerkraut is a staple, made by fermenting cabbage with salt. Its tangy flavor and crisp texture make it a beloved side dish, condiment, and ingredient in dishes like stews and casseroles. Japan offers a variety of fermented products, including miso, which is known as a fermented soybean paste that is a foundation of Japanese cuisine, providing the base for miso soup and adding umami to a wide range of dishes. Soy sauce, another fermented soy product, is indispensable in Asian cooking, used as a seasoning and marinade.

It is commonly known that eating fermented food has health benefits. The food's nutritional profile is improved and preservation is achieved through the fermentation process. Probiotics, or good bacteria, are rich in fermented foods and help maintain a healthy gut microbiome. Better digestion, a more robust immune system, and a lower chance of developing specific chronic diseases are all associated with a balanced gut microbiome. Fermented foods are also known to increase the bioavailability of nutrients, making vitamins and minerals more accessible to the body. Additionally, they can be a good source of B vitamins, including B12, which is often lacking in vegetarian diets.

The cultural significance of fermented foods cannot be overstated. These foods are deeply embedded in the traditions and histories of the cultures that created them. Making kimchi, for instance, involves a communal activity known as "kimjang," where families and communities come together to prepare significant quantities of kimchi to last through the winter. This tradition is not only a way to preserve food but also to strengthen communal bonds and has been pass down cultural heritage from one generation to the next. Similarly, the making of sauerkraut, miso, and other fermented foods often involves traditional techniques and family recipes, reflecting the identity and continuity of cultures around the world.

The fermentation process itself is a fascinating interplay between nature and culture. It involves creating conditions that encourage the growth of beneficial microorganisms while inhibiting harmful ones. In the case of kimchi and sauerkraut, this is achieved through the salting of vegetables, which draws out water and creates an anaerobic environment conducive to fermentation. Miso and soy sauce involve the fermentation of soybeans with a specific type of mold that initiates the fermentation process. These methods showcase human ingenuity in harnessing natural processes for food preservation, flavor enhancement, and health promotion.

In conclusion, kimchi and other fermented delights are much more than culinary curiosities. They are a vibrant expression of cultural heritage, a testament to the wisdom of conventional food preservation methods, and a valuable source of nutrition and health benefits. The process of fermentation transforms simple ingredients into complex, flavorful foods that nourish both the body and the soul. As the interest in fermented foods continues to grow, driven by a desire for wholesome, natural foods and a curiosity about global cuisines, these ancient delicacies are finding new audiences and appreciation. Whether it is the spicy kick of kimchi, the tangy crunch of sauerkraut, or the umami depth of miso, fermented foods offer a delicious and healthful connection to the rich tapestry of human culture and culinary innovation.

Troubleshooting Common Issues

Fermentation is an ancient culinary art that has been practiced worldwide for centuries, revered for its ability to preserve food, enhance flavors, and imbue dishes with unique qualities. However, the process of fermenting foods can sometimes be as unpredictable as it is fascinating, leading to common issues that both novice and experienced fermenters may encounter. This section delves into troubleshooting these issues, exploring their causes and providing solutions to ensure successful fermentation projects.

One of the most common issues in fermentation is the development of mold. Mold can appear on the surface of ferments for several reasons, including exposure to air, insufficient salt concentration, or contamination. To prevent mold growth, it's crucial to ensure that the vegetables or fruits are completely submerged in the brine, creating an anaerobic (oxygen-free) environment where harmful molds cannot thrive. Using a clean weight to keep the produce submerged and covering the fermenting vessel with a cloth or a lid can help maintain this environment. If mold does appear, removing the affected area promptly and ensuring the rest of the ferment is still submerged can sometimes save the batch, provided the mold has not penetrated deeply.

Another challenge is the development of a slimy or mushy texture in fermented vegetables, which is often due to enzymes breaking down the vegetable tissues. This issue can be mitigated by using fresh, crisp produce and adding tannin-rich leaves such as grape, oak, or horseradish to the ferment, which help preserve the crunchiness of the vegetables. Additionally, controlling the fermentation temperature to prevent it from becoming too warm can also help maintain the desired texture, as higher temperatures can accelerate the fermentation process excessively.

Kahm yeast is a white, filmy layer that sometimes forms on the surface of ferments, particularly in slower or less acidic fermentations. While not harmful, kahm yeast can impart an off-flavor to the ferment. To avoid this, ensure the fermentation environment is as clean as possible and that the vegetables are fully submerged under the brine. If kahm yeast appears, it can be skimmed off the surface, and the ferment can still be consumed if it smells and tastes acceptable.

An overly sour or acidic flavor is another common issue, usually resulting from over-fermentation. To control the acidity level, taste the ferment regularly and transfer it to the refrigerator to slow down the fermentation process once it reaches the desired flavor. The cool temperatures of the fridge significantly slow microbial activity, helping to preserve the ferment's flavor at its peak.

Insufficiently sour or flavorful ferments can result from under-fermentation or an environment that is too cold, which inhibits microbial activity. Ensuring the ferment is kept at a consistent, appropriate temperature can address this issue. If the ferment is not developing as expected, moving it to a slightly warmer spot can encourage the fermentation process.

Sometimes, fermenters may encounter a lack of fizziness in fermented beverages like kombucha or kefir, which is often due to a lack of sugars for the yeast to consume or not enough time allowed for fermentation. Ensuring there is enough sugar and allowing more time can help develop the desired carbonation. Additionally, sealing the fermenting beverage in a bottle can help trap carbon dioxide produced during fermentation, increasing fizziness.

Salt concentration can significantly impact the success of a ferment. Too much salt can inhibit fermentation, while too little can fail to prevent the growth of undesirable microorganisms. It's essential to follow recipes closely or use a salt calculator specific to the type of ferment to ensure the correct balance. Adjusting the salt concentration can often salvage a ferment that is not progressing as expected.

Cross-contamination is a risk in any fermentation process, where unwanted bacteria or yeasts from the environment or utensils can introduce off-flavors or spoilage. Using clean, sterilized equipment and practicing good hygiene can minimize this risk. Additionally, using starter cultures, when appropriate, can help ensure the right microbes dominate the fermentation process.

Fermentation is as much an art as it is a science, with variables such as temperature, ingredient quality, and cleanliness playing significant roles in the outcome. Troubleshooting common issues in fermenting often requires patience, observation, and a willingness to experiment. By comprehending the underlying causes of these issues as well as implementing the suggested solutions, fermenters can navigate the challenges of fermentation, leading to successful and delicious fermented foods and beverages. Whether dealing with mold, texture problems, unwanted yeast, or flavor imbalances, the key is to create the optimal conditions for beneficial microbes to thrive, ensuring the preservation and enhancement of food through this ancient and enduring culinary practice.

CHAPTER V

Pickled Delights

Classic Dill Pickles

Classic dill pickles, a timeless favorite among pickle aficionados, epitomize the art of pickling with their crisp texture, tangy flavor, and aromatic dill infusion. These pickles are not just a condiment or a casual snack; they are a culinary tradition that spans cultures and generations, embodying the essence of pickling expertise. This section delves into the history, making, and cultural significance of classic dill pickles, offering insights into why they continue to be cherished worldwide.

The origin of dill pickles traces back to ancient times when the practice of pickling emerged as a necessity for preserving food. The technique of fermenting cucumbers with dill and other seasonings was honed over centuries, becoming a staple in many cuisines, notably Eastern European and Jewish traditions. The name "pickle" itself derives from the Dutch word "pekel" or the German "pökel," referring to a brine or marinade used in the pickling process. Dill pickles gained prominence for their unique combination of sour, salty, and herbaceous flavors, making them a versatile ingredient in various dishes and a delightful snack on their own.

The process of making classic dill pickles involves fermenting cucumbers in a water solution mixed with salt, vinegar, dill, and often garlic, mustard seeds, and other spices. The cucumbers are typically harvested during the peak of freshness in late summer, then washed and packed tightly in jars or barrels. The brine, crucial to the pickling process, acts as a preservative and flavoring agent, inhibiting the growth of harmful bacteria while promoting the fermentation of natural sugars in the cucumbers into lactic acid. This fermentation process is what gives dill pickles their characteristic tangy flavor and crisp texture.

Dill, the defining herb in classic dill pickles, imparts a distinctive, slightly sweet and grassy flavor that complements the tanginess of the vinegar and the saltiness of the brine. The choice of dill, whether fresh or dried, significantly influences the flavor profile of the pickles. Fresh dill tends to offer a more vibrant taste and aroma, while dried dill can provide a more concentrated flavor. The addition of garlic and mustard seeds adds depth and complexity to the pickles, with garlic offering a pungent kick and mustard seeds delivering a mild spiciness.

The cultural significance of classic dill pickles extends beyond their culinary use. In many Eastern European countries, dill pickles are a staple at holiday feasts and family gatherings, symbolizing hospitality and tradition. They are often served alongside hearty meals, complementing rich dishes with their refreshing tanginess. In the United States, dill pickles have become synonymous with barbecue cookouts and deli sandwiches, showcasing their versatility and widespread appeal. Furthermore, dill pickles hold a special place in Jewish cuisine, particularly in the form of kosher dill pickles, which are made in accordance with kosher dietary laws and feature a distinct garlic flavor profile.

The art of making classic dill pickles is cherished by many as a way to connect with cultural heritage and practice culinary craftsmanship. Home pickling has seen a resurgence in recent years, with individuals seeking to recreate the traditional flavors of their ancestors or experiment with new variations. The process of pickling at home allows for customization of flavors and the satisfaction of creating a product that can be enjoyed with family and friends.

Classic dill pickles also offer nutritional benefits, being low in calories and fat while providing a source of vitamins K and A, along with minerals like potassium and iron. The fermentation process can produce probiotics, beneficial bacteria that support gut health, although this is more common in naturally fermented pickles than those made with vinegar.

Despite the simplicity of their ingredients, classic dill pickles represent a rich tapestry of culinary history, showcasing the evolution of pickling techniques and the enduring popularity of this humble pickle. They are a testament to the power of simple, natural preservation methods in creating flavors that resonate across time and culture.

In conclusion, classic dill pickles are much more than a side dish or a snack; they are a cultural icon, steeped in history and tradition. From their ancient origins to their modern-day status as a beloved staple in cuisines around the world, dill pickles continue to captivate the palates of many. The process of making these pickles, characterized by the careful balance of cucumbers, dill, vinegar, and spices, is a testament to the art of pickling. Whether enjoyed on their own, served alongside a meal, or used as an ingredient in recipes, classic dill pickles remain a cherished culinary delight, embodying the essence of pickled perfection.

Bread and Butter Pickles

Bread and butter pickles, a uniquely American contribution to the world of pickling, are distinguished by their sweet and tangy flavor profile, a departure from the purely sour taste of traditional dill pickles. This delightful variant of pickled cucumber has become a staple in American cuisine, beloved for its versatility and distinctive taste. The origins, preparation methods, and culinary uses of bread and butter pickles paint a picture of a food item that is as rich in history as it is in flavor. This section explores the intricacies of bread and butter pickles, shedding light on their creation, evolution, and enduring popularity.

The story of bread and butter pickles is said to date back to the Great Depression in the United States. It is believed that Omar and Cora Fanning, Illinois cucumber farmers, traded these sweetly pickled cucumbers for groceries, including bread and butter, hence the name. However, the precise origin of the name remains a topic of culinary lore, with some suggesting it refers to the pickles' role as a staple sandwich complement, as ubiquitous and essential as bread and butter themselves. Regardless of their nomenclature's origins, these pickles quickly became a beloved part of American culinary tradition, offering a sweet reprieve during times of economic hardship.

The preparation of bread and butter pickles involves slicing cucumbers thinly and pickling them in a mixture of vinegar, sugar, and a distinctive blend of spices including mustard seeds, celery seeds, and turmeric. The addition of sugar to the vinegar brine creates the signature sweet-sour flavor profile, while the spices contribute a complex aroma and taste that set bread and butter pickles apart from their pickling counterparts. Turmeric, in particular, gives these pickles their characteristic bright yellow hue, making them not only delicious but also visually appealing.

The pickling process for bread and butter pickles is relatively straightforward, allowing for both amateur cooks and seasoned chefs to prepare them at home with ease. Typically, the cucumbers are first soaked in ice water to crisp them up before being combined with onions and the pickling brine. The mixture is then heated and poured into jars, where the pickles undergo a quick pickling process. This method ensures that the cucumbers retain their crispness, a crucial textural element of bread and butter pickles. Unlike fermented pickles, bread and butter pickles are ready to eat shortly after cooling, offering immediate gratification to those who make them.

Culinarily, bread and butter pickles are incredibly versatile, serving as both a condiment and an ingredient in various dishes. Their sweet tanginess makes them an ideal companion to sandwiches and burgers, providing a refreshing contrast to savory meats. They are also commonly used in potato salads, deviled eggs, and tuna salads, where they add a burst of flavor as well as a hint of sweetness. Moreover, the appeal of bread and butter pickles extends beyond the realm of savory dishes; they can also be a surprising yet delightful addition to sweet recipes, such as pickle-flavored ice creams or desserts, showcasing their flexibility in the culinary arts.

The popularity of bread and butter pickles lies not only in their taste and versatility but also in their ability to evoke nostalgia. For many, these pickles are reminiscent of childhood lunches, family picnics, and summer barbecues, embodying the simplicity and joy of American culinary traditions. The process of making bread and butter pickles at home, often using family recipes passed down through generations, strengthens these sentimental ties, making them more than just a food item but a cherished part of family heritage.

Nutritionally, bread and butter pickles offer several benefits. They are low in calories and fat, making them a guilt-free addition to any meal. However, due to their sugar content, they are higher in carbohydrates than their dill counterparts. Despite this, they still provide the health benefits associated with cucumbers, such as hydration and vitamins C and K. Moreover, like other pickled foods, bread and butter pickles contain vinegar, which has been associated to health benefits like enhanced digestion and blood sugar control.

Bread and butter pickles are a testament to the innovation and resilience of American culinary traditions. Born out of necessity during the Great Depression, these pickles have evolved into a beloved staple of American cuisine, celebrated for their unique sweet and tangy flavor. The simplicity of their preparation, combined with their culinary versatility, ensures their continued popularity among both home cooks and professional chefs. Beyond their taste, bread and butter pickles hold a special place in the hearts of many, serving as a symbol of family, tradition, and the comfort of home-cooked meals. As they continue to grace tables across the United States and beyond, bread and butter pickles stand as a flavorful reminder of the enduring appeal of pickled foods in American culture.

Pickled Onions

Pickled onions are a beloved condiment that transcends cultures, adding a piquant zest to dishes around the globe. This culinary delight, with its roots deep in the annals of culinary history, offers a tangy, sometimes sweet, counterpoint to the robust flavors of many traditional dishes. Through the simple act of pickling, onions are transformed from a sharp, often overpowering vegetable into a mellow, flavorful accompaniment that complements a wide array of culinary creations. This section explores the history, preparation, and culinary versatility of pickled onions, highlighting their unique position within the world's gastronomic traditions.

The practice of pickling onions is as ancient as it is widespread, with historical records suggesting that the technique dates back thousands of years. Ancient civilizations, recognizing the need to preserve surplus food for leaner times, utilized the natural preservative qualities of vinegar and salt to extend the shelf life of various foods, including onions. This method not only ensured a steady supply of onions throughout the year but also imbued them with distinct flavors that became integral to various culinary traditions. Over the centuries, pickled onions have become a staple in many cuisines, from the tangy, spice-infused onions found in Indian chutneys to the sweet and sour onions popular in British pubs.

The preparation of pickled onions begins with the selection of suitable onions. Small, firm onions are typically preferred for their crisp texture and mild flavor. These are peeled and sometimes scored or sliced before being submerged in a pickling solution. The brine, a crucial component of the pickling process, is a mixture of vinegar, water, salt, and often sugar, heated and poured over the onions. Spices including mustard seeds, peppercorns, and bay leaves are frequently added to the brine, infusing the onions with complex flavors as they pickle.

One of the most appealing aspects of pickled onions is their versatility. They can be personalized to suit a wide range of palates and dishes, with variations in the type of vinegar, the addition of sweeteners, and the choice of spices leading to dramatically different flavor profiles. For instance, using malt vinegar and a touch of sugar yields the classic British-style pickled onion, beloved for its robust, tangy flavor that pairs exceptionally well with strong cheeses and cold meats. Conversely, using white vinegar and an assortment of Indian spices can produce a pickled onion that is both piquant and aromatic, perfect for complementing the rich, spicy flavors of South Asian cuisine.

The culinary uses of pickled onions are as diverse as their preparation methods. They are often served as an accompaniment to meals, providing a bright, acidic contrast that enhances the flavors of the main dish. In Mexico, pickled red onions add a vibrant splash of color and a sharp, tangy flavor to tacos and cochinita pibil, while in Scandinavia, pickled onions are a key component of the traditional smorgasbord. Beyond their role as a condiment, pickled onions are also used as an ingredient in cooking, lending depth and acidity to stews, salads, and sandwiches.

Beyond their culinary appeal, pickled onions offer several health benefits. Onions themselves are rich in vitamins and antioxidants, and the pickling process can help preserve these nutrients. Additionally, vinegar, a key ingredient in the pickling brine, has been associated with various health benefits, including improved digestion and blood sugar control. However, it's worth noting that pickled onions also has high levels of sodium, so they should be consumed in moderation, especially by those monitoring their salt intake.

Despite the simplicity of their ingredients, making pickled onions is an art that requires attention to detail. The strength of the vinegar, the ratio of sugar to salt, and the pickling time all play crucial roles in determining the final flavor and texture of the onions. Achieving the perfect balance between acidity, sweetness, and spice is often a matter of personal taste, and many families have their cherished recipes passed down through generations. This personal touch adds to the appeal of pickled onions, making them not just a food item but a reflection of cultural and familial heritage.

In conclusion, pickled onions are a testament to the transformative power of pickling, a process that turns a simple vegetable into a versatile, flavorful condiment that enhances dishes across various cuisines. From their historical roots in ancient preservation techniques to their modern-day role as a gourmet addition to artisanal cheese boards and street food alike, pickled onions embody the complexity and diversity of global culinary traditions. Whether enjoyed as a tangy snack, a bright addition to salads, or a piquant topping for hearty mains, pickled onions continue to delight palates with their unique balance of flavors, proving that sometimes, the easiest ingredients can lead to the most extraordinary results.

Creative Pickling Recipes

Creative pickling recipes have transcended traditional boundaries, introducing a world where virtually any ingredient can be pickled, leading to an explosion of flavors, textures, and culinary possibilities. This exploration of innovative pickling extends beyond cucumbers and onions, venturing into fruits, flowers, and even meats, embodying the essence of culinary creativity and experimentation. This section delves into the realm of creative pickling, showcasing unique recipes that highlight the versatility and adaptability of pickling as a cooking method, and its ability to change ordinary ingredients into extraordinary culinary delights.

The art of pickling, at its core, is about preservation. However, modern culinary practices have elevated it to a form of gastronomic artistry, where the acidic tang of vinegar or the lactic acid from fermentation can enhance the natural flavors of ingredients, adding depth and complexity to dishes. Among the myriad of creative pickling recipes, some stand out for their ingenuity and flavor profiles, pushing the boundaries of what can be pickled and how these pickled goods can be used in everyday cooking.

One such recipe involves pickling watermelon rinds, a practice that transforms what is typically discarded into a sweet, tangy, and crisp treat. This recipe exemplifies sustainability in cooking, utilizing the entire fruit to minimize waste. The process involves removing the hard outer skin and pickling the white part of the rind in a brine made from vinegar, sugar, as well as a blend of spices like cloves, cinnamon, and allspice. The result is a surprisingly delightful pickle that bridges the gap between sweet and savory, perfect for adding a unique twist to salads or serving as a quirky accompaniment to grilled meats.

Another creative pickling endeavor is the preparation of pickled grapes. This recipe challenges preconceived notions about what fruits are suitable for pickling, offering a sweet and sour snack that's as delicious as it is unexpected. To create pickled grapes, small, seedless grapes are submerged in a brine of white wine vinegar, sugar, and aromatic spices such as mustard seeds, cinnamon sticks, and peppercorns. After a few days, the grapes take on a nuanced flavor profile that is both refreshing and complex, making them an excellent addition to cheese boards or as a garnish for cocktails.

Venturing further into the realm of creative pickling, some chefs and home cooks alike have begun to experiment with pickled strawberries. This delicacy involves soaking ripe strawberries in a mixture of balsamic vinegar, water, and sugar, along with fresh herbs like thyme or basil. The acidity of the vinegar amplifies the strawberries' natural sweetness while adding a layer of sophistication to their flavor. Pickled strawberries can elevate a simple dessert, add an intriguing element to salads, or serve as a captivating topping for vanilla ice cream.

Moving beyond fruits and vegetables, the concept of pickling can also extend to proteins, as evidenced by the traditional Scandinavian dish, pickled herring. This recipe showcases the versatility of pickling in preserving and flavoring fish. Herring fillets are cured in a brine of vinegar, sugar, onions, and spices, then left to marinate for several days. The result is a delicacy that is rich in flavor, with a tender texture and a balance of sweetness and acidity. Pickled herring is often served with dark rye bread, sour cream, and boiled potatoes, offering a glimpse into the cultural heritage of Scandinavian cuisine.

Creative pickling does not stop at solid foods; it also encompasses liquids. An innovative example is the pickling of juices, such as beet juice or tomato juice, which can be used as a base for brines or as an ingredient in vinaigrettes and marinades. These pickled juices retain the essence of their original ingredients while incorporating the complex flavors developed through the pickling process, adding a vibrant splash of color and taste to dishes.

The exploration of creative pickling recipes reflects a broader trend in contemporary cuisine towards experimentation and sustainability. By pushing the boundaries of traditional pickling, chefs and home cooks are not only able to discover new flavor combinations but also promote a more mindful approach to cooking, where waste is minimized, and every part of an ingredient is valued. These recipes encourage a playful engagement with food, inviting individuals to experiment with pickling various ingredients and to incorporate these pickled goods into their cooking repertoire in innovative ways.

In conclusion, the world of creative pickling is vast and varied, offering endless opportunities for culinary exploration. From the sweet crunch of pickled watermelon rinds to the savory depth of pickled herring, these recipes demonstrate the transformative power of pickling. Not only do they challenge our perceptions of what can be pickled, but they also provide a means to enhance the flavors and textures of dishes, contributing to a richer, more diverse culinary landscape. As more people embrace the art of pickling, it is clear that this ancient method of preservation will continue to inspire creativity in kitchens around the world, proving that the possibilities of pickling are limited only by the imagination.

CHAPTER VI

Beyond Vegetables

Fermented Beverages (Kombucha, Kefir)

Fermented beverages, like kombucha and kefir, have surged in popularity in recent years, celebrated not only for their unique flavors but also for their purported health benefits. These drinks, which have their origins in ancient cultures, are enjoying a renaissance in the modern health and wellness landscape, embodying the confluence of tradition, science, and the art of fermentation. This section explores the rich history, preparation methods, health benefits, and cultural significance of kombucha and kefir, shedding light on why these fermented beverages continue to captivate the interest of health enthusiasts and culinary adventurers alike.

Kombucha, often referred to as "mushroom tea," despite not containing actual mushrooms, is a fermented tea beverage that traces its origins to ancient China, where it was prized for its healing properties as far back as 220 B.C. The drink is produced by fermenting sweetened tea with a SCOBY also known as symbiotic culture of bacteria and yeast, which change the tea into a slightly effervescent, tangy beverage over the course of several days or weeks. The SCOBY, a gelatinous, pancake-like disc, consumes the sugar in the tea, producing a variety of acids, vitamins, and trace amounts of alcohol in the process. This fermentation not only imparts kombucha with its distinctive taste but also enriches it with probiotics, beneficial compounds that are thought to contribute to gut health and overall well-being.

Kefir, on the other hand, has its roots in the Caucasus Mountains, where it has been taken in for thousands of years. This fermented milk drink is made using kefir grains, a complex matrix of bacteria and yeasts, which ferment the lactose in milk, turning it into a tangy, slightly carbonated beverage that is thinner than yogurt. Kefir grains look somewhat like cauliflower florets but are gelatinous in texture. The fermentation process not only breaks down the lactose, making kefir simpler to digest for those with lactose intolerance but also infuses the milk with probiotics, vitamins, and minerals. Like kombucha, kefir is believed to offer many health benefits, like improved digestion and enhanced immune function.

The preparation of both kombucha and kefir involves a fascinating interplay of microbial activity, where the environment, temperature, and time play crucial roles in shaping the final product's flavor and nutritional profile. For kombucha, the process begins with brewing a batch of tea, sweetening it, and then adding the SCOBY to the cooled liquid. The mixture is then covered with a cloth and left to ferment at room temperature for anywhere from a week to a month, depending on the desired level of acidity. Making kefir is combining milk with kefir grains and letting it ferment for approximately a day at room temperature. After fermentation, the kefir is ready to be drank or refrigerated, and the grains are strained out and can be used again for later batches.

The probiotic content of kombucha and kefir is largely responsible for their numerous health benefits. Probiotics are live bacteria that give health advantages to the host when taken in sufficient doses, especially for digestive health. Probiotics found in kombucha and kefir help to keep a healthy balance of gut bacteria, which can improve immune system function, improve nutrient absorption, and possibly lower the risk of some digestive problems. Additionally, these beverages contain various acids, enzymes, and antioxidants that may contribute to detoxification processes and overall health.

Beyond their health benefits, kombucha and kefir hold significant cultural importance in their regions of origin, where they have been passed down through generations as traditional remedies and celebratory drinks. In recent years, this cultural heritage has been embraced by a global audience, leading to a proliferation of commercial and home-brewed versions of these beverages. The growing interest in fermented foods and beverages, driven by a broader trend towards natural, functional, and gut-friendly products, has positioned kombucha and kefir as staples in the diet of health-conscious consumers.

Despite their ancient origins, kombucha and kefir are highly adaptable to modern tastes, with numerous variations and flavors available. Kombucha can be infused with fruits, herbs, and spices during a second fermentation process to create a wide range of flavors, from ginger-lemon to raspberry-mint. Similarly, kefir can be flavored with fruit purees or vanilla extract, or used as a base for smoothies and other culinary creations. This versatility, combined with their health benefits and rich histories, contributes to the enduring appeal of kombucha and kefir.

In conclusion, kombucha and kefir exemplify the enduring value of fermented beverages, bridging the gap between ancient wisdom and contemporary health trends. Their complex flavors, nutritional benefits, and the fascinating processes involved in their production speak to the human capacity for innovation in the pursuit of well-being. As research continues to uncover the many ways in which gut health influences overall health, it is likely that the popularity of kombucha, kefir, and other probiotic-rich foods and beverages will continue to grow. Through the lens of these fermented drinks, we gain insight into the power of fermentation to transform simple ingredients into nourishing elixirs that nourish the body, delight the palate, and connect us to our cultural heritage.

Fermented Condiments (Soy Sauce, Fish Sauce)

Fermented condiments, such as soy sauce and fish sauce, are culinary staples that have played a pivotal role in the world's cuisines for centuries. These ancient creations are the products of a natural fermentation process that transforms simple ingredients into complex and intensely flavored seasonings. Soy sauce, originating in China, and fish sauce, tracing its roots to Southeast Asia, are revered for their umami-rich profiles and their ability to enhance the flavors of countless dishes. This section explores the fascinating histories, production methods, flavor profiles, and cultural significance of these fermented condiments, shedding light on why they continue to be revered and integrated into global culinary traditions.

Soy sauce, also known as shoyu in Japan, is believed to have originated in China over 2,500 years ago during the Zhou dynasty. It is made from soybeans, wheat, salt, and water, and the process of soy sauce production involves a unique fermentation called "koji." Koji is a mold (Aspergillus oryzae) that is cultivated on steamed soybeans and wheat, breaking down starches into sugars. This koji mixture is combined with brine and left to ferment for months or even years, allowing a complex transformation to occur. The result is a dark, salty, and umami-rich liquid that ranges in flavor from light and delicate to robust and intense, depending on the length of fermentation and the specific production methods.

Fish sauce, on the other hand, boasts origins in ancient Southeast Asia, with early records dating back to the 2nd century AD. It is made by fermenting fish, usually anchovies or other small varieties, with salt. The fish are layered with salt in barrels or containers and left to ferment for several months. Over time, enzymes and microbes break down the fish proteins and turn them into amino acids, giving fish sauce its signature savory, salty, and pungent flavor. The liquid is then extracted, strained, and sometimes aged further to develop its complexity.

Both soy sauce and fish sauce are celebrated for their umami qualities, which enhance the depth and savoriness of dishes. Umami, often defined as the fifth taste alongside sweet, sour, salty, and bitter, is responsible for the rich, satisfying flavors found in foods like aged cheeses, mushrooms, and ripe tomatoes. Soy sauce's umami comes from the breakdown of soybean proteins into amino acids during fermentation, while fish sauce's umami originates from the hydrolysis of fish proteins.

The significance of these fermented condiments extends far beyond their flavor profiles. They have become indispensable in the culinary traditions of the regions where they originated and have been adopted and adapted in cuisines worldwide. In Japan, soy sauce is an integral part of dishes such as sushi, sashimi, and teriyaki, contributing a balance of saltiness and umami. In Southeast Asian cuisine, fish sauce is known as a fundamental ingredient, lending its salty depth to dishes like pad Thai, green papaya salad, and Vietnamese pho. These condiments are also valued for their ability to impart complexity and depth of flavor to vegetarian and vegan dishes, where umami-rich ingredients are prized.

The cultural significance of these condiments extends beyond the kitchen. They are often symbolic of culinary heritage and regional identity. In Japan, for example, soy sauce production is a deeply ingrained tradition, with different regions producing their own unique varieties, each with distinct flavor profiles. In Thailand, fish sauce is considered a national treasure, and artisanal production methods are passed down through generations. These condiments are also associated with ritual and ceremony, such as the use of soy sauce in Japanese tea ceremonies or the inclusion of fish sauce in Southeast Asian culinary celebrations.

From a health perspective, fermented condiments like soy sauce and fish sauce offer several benefits. Their fermentation process breaks down proteins, making them easier to digest, and can increase the bioavailability of certain nutrients. Additionally, they contain naturally occurring probiotics, beneficial bacteria that can support gut health. However, it's important to use these condiments in moderation due to their high salt content, especially for individuals with hypertension or other dietary restrictions.

In conclusion, fermented condiments like soy sauce and fish sauce are more than just seasonings; they are cultural treasures with rich histories and profound culinary importance. Their umami-rich flavors enhance a wide range of dishes and have found a place in kitchens around the world. As the appreciation for umami continues to grow, these fermented condiments remain essential in creating the complex, satisfying flavors that define global cuisine. They serve as a testament to the transformative power of fermentation, where simple ingredients are elevated to the level of culinary artistry, enriching our culinary experiences and connecting us to the traditions and flavors of the past.

Fermented Dairy (Yogurt, Cheese)

Fermented dairy products, including yogurt and cheese, represent some of the oldest and most beloved culinary creations in human history. These dairy marvels are the result of carefully controlled microbial transformations, where milk undergoes fermentation, producing a wide array of textures and flavors. Yogurt, which originated thousands of years ago in regions such as Mesopotamia and the Middle East, is a creamy as well as tangy delight that offers many health benefits. Cheese, with its origins dating back over 7,000 years, takes milk to entirely new dimensions, ranging from soft and fresh to aged and sharp. This section explores the rich history, production methods, diverse varieties, and the significant cultural and nutritional roles of yogurt and cheese, shedding light on their enduring appeal in global cuisine.

Yogurt, a probiotic-rich dairy product, has been enjoyed by various cultures throughout history. Its roots can be originated back to ancient civilizations in the Middle East and the Mediterranean, where the practice of fermenting milk to produce yogurt was first discovered. The process of yogurt-making involves the introduction of specific bacterial cultures, primarily Lactobacillus bulgaricus and Streptococcus thermophilus, into milk. These bacteria consume the lactose in milk, converting it to lactic acid, which thickens the milk as well as gives yogurt its characteristic tangy flavor. The result is a creamy, custard-like substance that is not only delicious but also rich in probiotics, live beneficial bacteria that are known to support digestive health and to boost the immune system.

Yogurt's global popularity can be attributed to its versatility and adaptability in culinary applications. It can be enjoyed plain or with an array of toppings, such as honey, fruit, nuts, or granola. Yogurt's creamy texture and tangy taste also make it a versatile ingredient in both sweet as well as savory dishes. In Mediterranean cuisine, it is used to make tzatziki, a refreshing cucumber and yogurt dip, while Indian cuisine features raita, a yogurt-based side dish often served with spicy curries. The probiotic nature of yogurt has contributed to its reputation as a health food, as it is believed to aid in digestion and enhance gut health.

Cheese, on the other hand, is a dairy product that undergoes a complex transformation, with variations in taste, texture, and aroma that span a wide spectrum. The origins of cheese can be tracked to regions across the Middle East, Europe, and Asia, where the practice of curdling milk to separate curds and whey gave rise to a diverse array of cheeses. The basic cheese-making process involves coagulating milk with the addition of acid (like lemon juice or vinegar) or enzymes (usually derived from calf rennet or microbial sources) to form curds. These curds are then drained and pressed, resulting in the formation of cheese.

The world of cheese is incredibly diverse, encompassing countless varieties, each with its unique characteristics. Soft, fresh cheeses like mozzarella and feta are mild and creamy, often used in salads and pasta dishes. Semi-soft cheeses like cheddar and Gouda have a pliable texture and a wide range of flavors, from mild and buttery to sharp and nutty. Hard cheeses including Parmesan and Pecorino Romano are dense and crumbly, characterized by intense flavors that intensify with age. Blue cheeses like Roquefort and Gorgonzola develop blue veins of mold, which impart a distinctive tangy and pungent flavor.

The production of cheese is not only about creating an array of flavors and textures but also about preserving milk for longer periods. The fermentation process in cheese-making involves the conversion of lactose into lactic acid and other compounds, which act as natural preservatives. This has allowed cheese to become a staple food in many cultures, providing a source of nutrition and sustenance over extended periods.

Beyond their culinary significance, yogurt and cheese hold cultural importance in various regions around the world. In Greece, yogurt is revered for its creamy texture and tart flavor, serving as the foundation for dishes like moussaka and Greek salad. In Italy, cheese is an integral part of the cultural and culinary identity, with Parmigiano-Reggiano and mozzarella being recognized and protected by designations of origin. Cheese has also played a prominent role in European monastic traditions, with monks often being credited with developing and perfecting cheese-making techniques.

From a nutritional standpoint, both yogurt and cheese offer a range of health benefits. Probiotics, which can enhance gut health and aid in digestion, are included in yogurt along with protein and calcium. In addition, it offers vital minerals and vitamins like riboflavin and vitamin B12. Cheese, similarly, is rich in protein and calcium, making it a valuable addition to the diet. Aged cheeses, in particular, are known for their high concentration of vitamins as well as minerals, like vitamin K2, which plays a part in bone health.

In conclusion, yogurt and cheese are two dairy products that exemplify the extraordinary diversity of flavors and textures that can be achieved through fermentation. They have become integral components of cuisines around the world, each with its unique cultural significance and culinary applications. Beyond their delectable taste, yogurt and cheese offer valuable nutritional benefits, contributing to overall health and well-being. As these fermented dairy products continue to evolve and adapt to modern tastes, they serve as a testament to the enduring appeal of age-old traditions in the realm of food and gastronomy.

CHAPTER VII

Safety and Preservation

Food Safety Guidelines

Food safety guidelines for fermented and pickled foods are paramount to ensure the preservation of quality, taste, and safety in these unique culinary creations. Fermentation and pickling have been traditional methods of food preservation for centuries, relying on the natural process of microbial transformation to enhance flavor and extend shelf life. However, it is crucial to follow stringent food safety practices to harness the benefits of fermentation and pickling while minimizing the risks of foodborne illnesses and spoilage. This section explores the specific food safety considerations for fermented and pickled foods, covering key aspects such as hygiene, ingredient quality, temperature control, and safe processing methods.

The foundation of food safety in fermented and pickled foods begins with strict hygiene practices. Cleanliness is paramount, and this applies to both the environment and the individuals involved in the preparation process. To avoid the introduction of harmful bacteria, all surfaces, utensils, as well as equipment used in the preparation of these foods must be carefully cleaned and sterilized. Food handlers need to maintain proper personal hygiene, which includes often washing their hands with soap and water. This is especially crucial because hands might introduce contaminants that have an impact on the finished product.

Another important factor to consider is the quality of the ingredients used in fermented and pickled dishes. Fresh, high-quality ingredients are necessary to guarantee the finished product's safety and flavor. Fresh produce should be free from visible signs of spoilage or damage, and meats should be of good quality and properly stored. Additionally, the water used in the fermentation or pickling process should be safe and free from contaminants. Any ingredients that are past their prime or of questionable quality should be avoided to prevent the introduction of pathogens or undesirable flavors.

Temperature control is a key factor in food safety for fermented and pickled foods. Temperature influence the rate of microbial activity and can determine whether fermentation proceeds safely or leads to spoilage. It is essential to maintain ingredients within safe temperature ranges throughout the fermentation or pickling process. For instance, when fermenting vegetables, it is crucial to keep them submerged in brine and at a temperature between 60°F (15°C) and 70°F (21°C) to encourage the growth of beneficial lactic acid bacteria while inhibiting harmful microorganisms. Failure to control temperature can result in undesirable microbial growth or spoilage, leading to unsafe or unpalatable products.

The use of salt and acid is a fundamental aspect of food safety in fermented and pickled foods. Salt serves as a preservative by creating an environment that is less hospitable to spoilage microorganisms. In some cases, such as sauerkraut and kimchi, salt is used to draw moisture from vegetables, creating an environment conducive to lactic acid fermentation. Acid, usually in the form of vinegar or citrus juice, plays a similar role by lowering the pH of the pickling liquid, inhibiting the growth of harmful bacteria. Properly measuring and adding the correct amount of salt and acid is crucial to achieve the desired preservation and flavor in these foods.

To ensure food safety in fermented and pickled foods, it is important to follow safe processing methods. This includes using clean and sterilized containers for fermentation or pickling, sealing them tightly to prevent contamination, and providing proper ventilation to release excess gas produced during fermentation. When canning pickled products for long-term storage, safe canning techniques must be employed. This involves using sterilized jars, maintaining appropriate headspace, and following recommended canning methods, such as water bath or pressure canning, depending on the specific product and recipe. Adhering to established canning procedures is critical to prevent the risk of botulism and other foodborne illnesses.

Labeling and record-keeping are additional food safety practices that can enhance the safety of fermented and pickled foods. Clearly labeling containers with the date of production and the type of food can help track freshness and identify any batches that may have issues. Maintaining records of recipes, ingredient sources, and processing methods can be invaluable in case of any safety concerns or recalls.

Consumer education is also a vital component of food safety for fermented and pickled foods. Educating consumers about safe handling practices, including refrigeration and proper storage, can help prevent foodborne illnesses. Providing clear instructions on the shelf life of products and how to recognize signs of spoilage or contamination is essential for consumer safety.

In conclusion, food safety guidelines for fermented and pickled foods are essential to ensure the preservation of quality, flavor, and safety in these time-honored culinary creations. Hygiene, ingredient quality, temperature control, salt and acid use, safe processing methods, labeling, and consumer education are all critical aspects of food safety that must be adhered to throughout the production and consumption of these foods. By following these guidelines, individuals and producers can continue to enjoy the unique and delicious flavors of fermented and pickled foods while safeguarding against the risks of foodborne illnesses and spoilage. Food safety is not only a matter of tradition but also a fundamental commitment to the well-being of those who savor these culinary treasures.

Storing Fermented and Pickled Foods

Storing fermented and pickled foods is a critical aspect of preserving their quality, flavor, and safety. These ancient preservation techniques have been utilized for centuries to lengthen the shelf life of perishable ingredients, enhance their taste, and create unique culinary delights. Whether it's sauerkraut, kimchi, pickles, or other fermented and pickled products, proper storage is essential to maintain their characteristics and prevent spoilage or foodborne illnesses. This section explores the importance of storing fermented and pickled foods, the factors that influence their shelf life, and the best practices for ensuring their longevity and safety.

Fermented and pickled foods owe their longevity to the transformation brought about by microbial activity during the fermentation process. Beneficial bacteria, such as lactobacilli, convert sugars and starches into lactic acid and other organic compounds, creating an acidic environment that hinders the growth of harmful microorganisms. This acidity not only acts as a natural preservative but also contributes to the distinctive flavors and tanginess of these foods. However, once the fermentation process is complete, proper storage becomes crucial to maintain these qualities and prevent the growth of spoilage bacteria and molds.

One of the primary factors influencing the shelf life of fermented and pickled foods is temperature. Storing these foods at the right temperature can significantly extend their freshness. In general, most fermented and pickled products should be kept in a cool, dark place, away from direct sunlight and temperature fluctuations. Refrigeration is often recommended for fermented products like sauerkraut, kimchi, and yogurt, as lower temperatures slow down microbial activity and help preserve the products' texture and flavor. But because the pickling liquid is acidic, some pickled goods, like cucumbers pickled in vinegar, can be kept at room temperature without risk.

The type of container used is another important factor to consider while storing fermented and pickled foods. In order to keep these meals from rotting due to oxygen exposure, they are usually kept in airtight containers. Commonly used for this purpose are glass jars, ceramic crocks, or as food-grade plastic containers with tight-fitting lids. The choice of container should also be non-reactive to avoid any adverse chemical reactions with the acidic nature of the pickled or fermented product.

In addition to temperature and container choice, the duration of storage is a key aspect to consider. Fermented and pickled foods have varying shelf lives depending on factors such as their acidity, salt content, and the presence of preservatives. High-acid products like vinegar-pickled vegetables can be stored for an extended period, often several months to a year, without significant quality loss. In contrast, lower-acid items like sauerkraut and kimchi may have shorter shelf lives, typically ranging from a few weeks to a few months. It's important to check the product's label or refer to a trusted recipe for guidance on storage duration.

Proper sealing and handling are essential when storing fermented and pickled foods. Any container used should be thoroughly cleaned and sanitized before filling it with the product. The lid or cover should be securely tightened to create an airtight seal. If the product is stored in a brine or pickling liquid, the food items should be fully submerged to prevent mold growth. Any signs of spoilage, such as off odors, changes in texture, or mold growth, should be taken seriously, and the affected portion should be discarded to prevent contamination of the entire batch.

When using home canning methods to store pickled products, it's crucial to follow tested and trusted recipes and canning procedures to ensure safety. Proper canning involves the use of sterilized jars, appropriate headspace, and a water bath or pressure canner to destroy any remaining harmful microorganisms. Following established canning guidelines reduces the risk of botulism and other foodborne illnesses associated with improperly canned products.

In conclusion, storing fermented and pickled foods is a crucial aspect of preserving their quality, flavor, and safety. These foods, enriched by microbial activity during fermentation, offer unique taste experiences and the potential for extended shelf life. Factors such as temperature, container choice, duration of storage, and proper sealing play pivotal roles in ensuring the longevity as well as safety of these products. Whether in a home kitchen or a commercial setting, adherence to proper storage practices is essential to savor the rich flavors and benefits of fermented and pickled foods while avoiding the risks of spoilage or foodborne illness. By respecting the traditions of preservation and embracing modern food safety standards, we can continue to enjoy the timeless pleasures of these culinary treasures.

Extending Shelf Life

Extending the shelf life of fermented and pickled foods is a key objective for both home cooks and commercial producers. These time-honored preservation methods offer a unique array of flavors and textures, but ensuring that these products remain safe and flavorful over time requires careful attention to various factors. From the choice of ingredients and processing techniques to storage conditions and packaging, several strategies can be employed to prolong the shelf life of fermented and pickled foods. This section delves into the importance of shelf life extension, the factors influencing it, and the best practices that can be used to maximize the quality and safety of these beloved culinary creations.

Shelf life extension is a critical consideration for fermented and pickled foods due to their perishable nature. These foods undergo natural microbial transformations during fermentation and pickling, which, if not controlled, can lead to spoilage or the growth of harmful microorganisms. Therefore, the primary goal of extending shelf life is to maintain the safety and quality of these products for an extended period, allowing consumers to savor their flavors and reap their nutritional benefits.

One of the most crucial factors influencing the shelf life of fermented and pickled foods is the choice of ingredients. Fresh and high-quality ingredients are essential to ensure the longevity of the final product. Produce should be free from visible signs of spoilage or damage, and meats should be of good quality and properly handled. Moreover, the water used in the preparation of brines or pickling solutions should be clean and free from contaminants. Any ingredients that are past their prime or of questionable quality should be avoided to prevent the introduction of pathogens or undesirable flavors.

Proper processing techniques are another key aspect of shelf life extension. Fermentation and pickling involve controlling microbial activity to achieve specific flavor profiles and prevent spoilage. The use of salt, acid (such as vinegar), and sometimes sugar serves as both a preservative and a flavor enhancer. The concentration of these elements in the brine or pickling solution must be carefully measured and adjusted to create an environment that inhibits the growth of harmful microorganisms while promoting the growth of beneficial ones. Achieving the right balance of salt, acid, and sugar is crucial to both preservation and taste.

Temperature control plays a significant role in extending the shelf life of fermented and pickled foods. Temperature influence the rate of microbial activity, and maintaining the products within safe temperature ranges is essential. In most cases, fermentation and pickling occur at room temperature or slightly cooler. Once the desired level of fermentation or pickling is achieved, the products are often moved to a cooler environment, such as a refrigerator or cellar, to slow down microbial activity and preserve their quality. Proper temperature control throughout the production and storage process is essential to prevent spoilage and maintain the desired flavors and textures.

Packaging and storage conditions also influence the shelf life of fermented and pickled foods. The choice of containers and packaging materials can impact the product's exposure to oxygen, which can lead to spoilage. Airtight containers, like glass jars with tightly sealed lids, are commonly used for storage to prevent oxygen from entering and affecting the product. It is also important to ensure that the food items are fully submerged in the pickling liquid or brine to avoid mold growth on the surface. Proper labeling with the date of production and product type can help track freshness and identify batches that may need to be consumed or discarded.

In commercial settings, there are additional techniques for shelf life extension, such as pasteurization or heat treatment. These processes involve heating the product to a specific temperature for a predetermined period to destroy any remaining harmful microorganisms and enzymes that can lead to spoilage. Pasteurization can extend the shelf life of certain products, but it may also affect their texture and flavor, so it is not always suitable for all fermented or pickled foods.

Consumer education is a critical component of shelf life extension. Educating consumers about proper storage, handling, and recognizing signs of spoilage or contamination is essential to ensure the safety of these products. Providing clear instructions on the shelf life of products and how to store them can help consumers maximize the longevity of their fermented and pickled foods.

In conclusion, extending the shelf life of fermented and pickled foods is a crucial aspect of preserving their quality, flavor, and safety. Careful consideration of ingredient quality, processing techniques, temperature control, packaging, and storage conditions is essential to achieve this goal. Whether in a home kitchen or a commercial setting, adherence to best practices in shelf life extension allows individuals and producers to enjoy the unique and delicious flavors of fermented and pickled foods while safeguarding against the risks of spoilage or foodborne illness. It is a testament to the enduring appeal of these culinary treasures and the commitment to preserving tradition and taste over time.

Reducing Food Waste

Reducing food waste for fermented and pickled foods is not only an ethical and environmental imperative but also a practical way to maximize the benefits of these traditional preservation methods. Fermentation and pickling have long been used to extend the shelf life of perishable ingredients, enhancing their flavors and creating unique culinary experiences. However, improper storage, overproduction, and lack of knowledge can lead to unnecessary food waste. This section explores the importance of minimizing food waste in the context of fermented and pickled foods, the factors contributing to waste, and strategies to reduce waste while enjoying the rich flavors and nutritional benefits of these beloved culinary creations.

Fermented and pickled foods have been valued for centuries for their ability to preserve ingredients and enhance their taste. However, preventing food waste in the context of these preservation methods is critical because it not only conserves valuable resources but also ensures that the efforts put into fermenting and pickling are not in vain. To achieve this, it is essential to understand the factors that contribute to food waste in this category and adopt strategies to mitigate them.

One of the primary contributors to food waste in fermented and pickled foods is overproduction. Many individuals and producers often prepare batches that are larger than needed, resulting in surplus products that may go to waste. To reduce overproduction, it is essential to plan carefully and consider portion sizes, especially when producing these foods on a larger scale. Understanding consumption patterns and adjusting production accordingly can help minimize surplus products that might eventually be discarded.

Improper storage is another significant factor leading to food waste. Fermented and pickled foods require specific storage conditions to maintain their quality and safety. Failure to store them appropriately can result in spoilage, rendering the products inedible. It is crucial to comply with the recommended storage guidelines, such as refrigeration or cool, dark storage, to extend the shelf life of these foods. Additionally, using airtight containers and ensuring that the food items are fully submerged in the pickling liquid or brine can prevent spoilage and mold growth.

Lack of knowledge about the shelf life and safe handling of fermented and pickled foods can also contribute to food waste. Consumers may discard products prematurely if they are unsure about their freshness or safety. To address this issue, it is essential to educate individuals about proper handling, storage, and the recognition of signs of spoilage. Providing clear labeling with the date of production and product type can help consumers make informed decisions about the safety and quality of these foods.

Another common cause of food waste in the context of fermented and pickled foods is neglecting to use less desirable parts of ingredients. For example, vegetable peels, stems, or leaves that are typically discarded can often be utilized in pickling or fermentation. These parts can add unique flavors and textures to the final product, reducing waste and making the most of the ingredients used. Creativity in using all edible portions of ingredients can not only minimize waste but also enhance the culinary experience.

To further minimize food waste in the production of fermented and pickled foods, it is essential to consider the scale of production. In commercial settings, batch sizes should be carefully calculated to match demand, reducing the likelihood of surplus products. Additionally, innovative approaches to using imperfect or surplus ingredients can be explored. For example, "ugly" or slightly damaged produce that may not be suitable for fresh consumption can be transformed into delicious pickled products, reducing food waste in the supply chain.

Consumer awareness and education are crucial in reducing food waste for fermented and pickled foods.

Promoting responsible consumption practices, such as portion control and using leftovers creatively, can help individuals make the most of these products. Consumers should also be encouraged to support local producers who prioritize sustainability and waste reduction in their production processes.

In conclusion, minimizing food waste for fermented and pickled foods is an essential endeavor that aligns with ethical, environmental, and practical considerations. Overproduction, improper storage, lack of knowledge, and neglecting to use less desirable parts of ingredients are common factors contributing to waste in this category. By adopting strategies such as careful planning, proper storage, education, and creative use of ingredients, individuals and producers can reduce food waste while savoring the rich flavors and nutritional benefits of fermented and pickled foods. This not only conserves resources but also honors the time-honored traditions of preservation and the value of every ingredient used.

CHAPTER VIII

Flavoring and Experimentation

Adding Herbs and Spices

Adding herbs and spices to fermented and pickled foods is a culinary art that elevates these traditional preservation methods to new heights. Herbs and spices not only infuse these foods with unique flavors but also contribute to their aroma, visual appeal, and even potential health benefits. Whether it's the dill in a classic dill pickle, the garlic in kimchi, or the juniper berries in sauerkraut, the use of herbs and spices enhances the complexity and depth of flavor in fermented and pickled creations. This section explores the significance of adding herbs and spices to these foods, the diverse range of options available, and the techniques for achieving the desired flavor profiles.

The practice of adding herbs as well as spices to fermented and pickled foods is rooted in both tradition and innovation. Throughout history, various cultures have developed their unique combinations of herbs and spices to create signature dishes. These additions not only impart distinct flavors but also reflect regional culinary traditions and preferences. For example, the use of dill, garlic, and mustard seeds in dill pickles is a hallmark of Eastern European pickling traditions, while the inclusion of ginger, garlic, and red pepper flakes characterizes Korean kimchi.

One of the primary reasons for adding herbs and spices to fermented and pickled foods is flavor enhancement. Herbs and spices introduce a diverse range of tastes, from the earthy warmth of cumin to the citrusy brightness of coriander. These flavors can complement and balance the inherent tanginess of fermented products or add complexity to the sweetness of pickled items. Herbs like thyme, rosemary, and basil can infuse a touch of freshness, while spices like cloves, cinnamon, and cardamom provide warmth and depth. The possibilities are endless, allowing chefs and home cooks to experiment and create unique taste experiences.

In addition to flavor, herbs and spices contribute to the aroma of fermented and pickled foods. The aromatic compounds present in these ingredients can create an enticing and appetizing fragrance that enhances the overall sensory experience. When a jar of pickles is opened, the scent of dill and garlic can be invigorating, while the earthy aroma of sauerkraut with juniper berries can evoke a sense of comfort. A well-balanced combination of herbs and spices not only pleases the palate but also tantalizes the nose.

Visual appeal is another aspect that herbs and spices bring to fermented and pickled foods. Ingredients like fresh dill sprigs, vibrant red chili peppers, or whole mustard seeds can add pops of color and texture to the final product. The visual contrast created by these additions not only makes the food more visually appealing but also signifies the unique flavor profiles within. The visual presentation of herbs and spices in fermented and pickled foods adds an element of excitement and anticipation for the consumer.

Beyond flavor, aroma, and visual appeal, herbs and spices used in fermented and pickled foods may offer potential health benefits. Numerous herbs and spices are known for their antioxidant properties and potential to enhance digestion. For example, ginger, a common addition to pickled products, is praised for its digestive benefits and anti-inflammatory properties. Turmeric, another spice often used in pickles, contains curcumin, a compound with potential health-promoting effects. While the quantities of these compounds in pickled products may be small, they contribute to the overall appeal of these foods as health-conscious choices.

The choice of herbs and spices for fermented and pickled foods is highly diverse, allowing for endless creativity and customization. Some herbs and spices are particularly well-suited for specific types of products. For example, dill, garlic, and mustard seeds are classic choices for cucumber pickles, while caraway seeds and juniper berries complement sauerkraut. In contrast, Asian pickled products like kimchi often feature ginger, garlic, and chili peppers. Herbs like thyme and oregano can enhance the flavor of pickled olives, while pickled beets benefit from the earthiness of cloves.

Achieving the desired flavor profile when adding herbs and spices to fermented and pickled foods requires some finesse. It is necessary to strike a balance to avoid overwhelming the natural flavors of the main ingredients. Measuring herbs and spices accurately and using them in appropriate quantities is key to achieving the desired taste. For example, a pinch of fresh dill may be sufficient for a small jar of pickles, while sauerkraut in a larger crock may require a few juniper berries for complexity.

The timing of adding herbs and spices is also crucial. Some herbs, such as delicate fresh herbs like basil or cilantro, are best added at the end of the fermentation or pickling process to preserve their freshness and aroma. Others, like robust dried spices or seeds, can be added at the beginning to allow their flavors to meld with the ingredients over time. Experimentation and tasting are essential to fine-tune the use of herbs and spices and achieve the desired balance of flavors.

In conclusion, the addition of herbs and spices to fermented and pickled foods is a culinary practice that enhances flavor, aroma, visual appeal, and even potential health benefits. These ingredients contribute to the complexity and depth of flavor in these traditional preservation methods, reflecting regional traditions and personal creativity. The careful selection and use of herbs and spices, along with attention to timing and balance, allow chefs and home cooks to create unique and memorable taste experiences in fermented and pickled dishes. From the spicy sting of chili peppers to the cozy embrace of cinnamon, herbs and spices bring a world of flavor to these beloved culinary creations.

Exploring Unique Flavor Combinations

Exploring unique flavor combinations for fermented and pickled foods is a delightful journey into the world of culinary creativity. Fermentation and pickling are age-old techniques that transform ordinary ingredients into extraordinary delights, and the addition of unexpected flavor pairings can elevate these traditional preservation methods to new heights. Whether it's the fusion of sweet and savory in a fruit-infused sauerkraut or the marriage of exotic spices in a pickled mango chutney, the possibilities are endless. This section delves into the significance of experimenting with unique flavor combinations in fermented and pickled foods, the diverse range of ingredients and techniques available, and the art of balancing flavors to create unforgettable taste experiences.

The exploration of unique flavor combinations in fermented and pickled foods is an exciting endeavor because it allows chefs and home cooks to break away from tradition and infuse their creations with personal creativity. While traditional recipes for fermented and pickled dishes have been passed down through generations, there is ample room for innovation. This innovation not only showcases the versatility of these preservation techniques but also reflects the diversity of ingredients and culinary traditions around the world.

One of the primary reasons for experimenting with unique flavor combinations is to create a sensory experience that surprises and delights the palate. By combining unexpected ingredients, such as herbs, spices, fruits, and vegetables, with the main ingredients, chefs and home cooks can craft dishes that offer a symphony of flavors. For example, adding slices of tart apples and a hint of cinnamon to a batch of sauerkraut can result in a sweet and savory masterpiece that pairs beautifully with a variety of dishes. Similarly, infusing pickled cucumbers with fresh dill and chili peppers can create a harmonious balance of coolness and heat.

The fusion of contrasting flavors is another aspect that makes unique combinations in fermented and pickled foods so appealing. The juxtaposition of sweet and sour, spicy and tangy, or savory and fruity can create a sensory experience that is both intriguing and memorable. For instance, pickling peaches with a blend of vinegar, sugar, and aromatic spices can result in a sweet and tangy condiment that pairs wonderfully with grilled meats or cheese. The interplay of these contrasting flavors adds depth and complexity to the dishes.

Exploring unique flavor combinations also allows for the incorporation of global influences into fermented and pickled foods. Culinary traditions from different regions of the world offer a treasure trove of ingredients and techniques that can be adapted to create innovative dishes. For example, the use of Korean gochugaru (red chili flakes) in pickling or the infusion of Indian spices like cumin and coriander into fermented vegetables can introduce exciting new dimensions to these foods. Embracing these global influences not only broadens culinary horizons but also celebrates the richness of food culture.

The process of achieving unique flavor combinations involves a careful selection of ingredients and a balance of flavors. It begins with a clear understanding of the main ingredient's characteristics and how it interacts with other elements. For example, when pickling cucumbers, it is essential to consider their inherent crispness and ability to absorb flavors. This knowledge informs the choice of complementary ingredients and techniques.

Balancing flavors in fermented and pickled foods is an art that involves the judicious use of sweet, salty, sour, and savory elements. Sugar or sweet fruits can provide sweetness, while salt or vinegar contributes saltiness and acidity. Herbs and spices add savory and aromatic notes. Achieving the desired balance requires tasting and adjusting the proportions of these elements to create a harmonious flavor profile. It is a process that requires both creativity and precision.

The timing of adding flavor ingredients is also crucial. Some elements, such as fresh herbs or delicate fruits, are best added towards the end of the fermentation or pickling process to preserve their freshness and aroma. Others, like dried spices or robust herbs, can be introduced earlier to allow their flavors to meld with the ingredients over time. Experimentation and tasting throughout the process are essential to fine-tune the balance and achieve the desired taste.

In conclusion, exploring unique flavor combinations in fermented and pickled foods is a culinary adventure that celebrates innovation and creativity. It allows chefs and home cooks to break away from tradition and infuse these time-honored preservation methods with a personal touch. The fusion of unexpected ingredients, the interplay of contrasting flavors, and the incorporation of global influences result in dishes that surprise and delight the palate. Achieving the perfect balance of sweet, salty, sour, and savory elements is an art that requires both knowledge and experimentation. From spicy mango pickles to herb-infused sauerkraut, the world of unique flavor combinations in fermented and pickled foods is a testament to the boundless possibilities of culinary exploration.

Customizing Your Ferments and Pickles

Customizing your ferments and pickles is a delightful culinary endeavor that allows individuals to tailor these traditional preservation methods to their unique tastes and preferences. Fermentation and pickling offer a canvas of possibilities, inviting creativity in ingredient selection, flavor profiles, and techniques. Whether it's adjusting the level of spiciness in kimchi, experimenting with diverse vegetables in mixed pickles, or infusing vinegar with aromatic herbs, customization allows for a personal touch in every batch. This section explores the significance of customizing ferments and pickles, the various aspects that can be tailored, and the techniques for achieving personalized culinary creations.

The act of customizing ferments and pickles is an expression of personal taste and culinary creativity. It allows individuals to move beyond standardized recipes and embrace the freedom of culinary experimentation. While traditional recipes for fermented and pickled foods have their merits, customization enables home cooks and chefs to craft dishes that resonate with their own flavor preferences and dietary needs.

One of the primary reasons for customizing ferments and pickles is to adjust the flavor profiles to one's liking. Everyone's palate is unique, and customization allows for the creation of dishes that cater to specific taste preferences. For example, adjusting the level of saltiness or sweetness in pickling solutions can make a significant difference in the final product's taste. Customization also empowers individuals to choose their preferred herbs, spices, and aromatics, resulting in flavor combinations that are personally satisfying.

Customization extends to ingredient selection as well. While traditional recipes often specify particular vegetables or fruits, there is room for creativity in choosing ingredients based on availability and personal preference. A mixed pickle, for instance, can be customized by selecting a diverse range of vegetables, each contributing its own texture and flavor to the medley. This flexibility allows for the use of seasonal produce or surplus ingredients, reducing food waste and promoting sustainability.

Customization in fermentation and pickling also considers dietary requirements and restrictions. For those with dietary sensitivities or preferences, such as gluten-free or vegan diets, customization allows for the exclusion of ingredients that may not align with those choices. Similarly, individuals can control the level of sweetness, sodium, or even the type of vinegar used to accommodate specific dietary needs.

The technique for customizing ferments and pickles involves a thoughtful consideration of the various elements involved in the process. It begins with an understanding of the main ingredient's characteristics and how it interacts with other components. For example, understanding the water content of vegetables or fruits is crucial in determining the appropriate level of saltiness in the pickling solution. Likewise, knowing how different herbs and spices complement or contrast with the main ingredient informs the selection and quantity of flavor enhancers.

The balance of flavors is a key aspect of customization. The interplay of sweet, salty, sour, and savory elements defines the taste of fermented and pickled foods. Customization allows individuals to adjust these elements to their preference. For example, a sweeter pickling solution can be achieved by adding more sugar or using sweet fruits like apples or pears. On the other hand, those who prefer a tangier profile can increase the acidity by using more vinegar or reducing the sugar content.

Customization also involves the selection of herbs, spices, and aromatics. These ingredients can significantly impact the flavor and aroma of the final product. Individuals can select from a huge array of options, ranging from classic choices like dill, garlic, and mustard seeds to more exotic selections like star anise, lemongrass, or juniper berries. Experimenting with different combinations and proportions allows for the creation of unique flavor profiles.

The timing of adding custom ingredients is another consideration. Some elements, such as fresh herbs, delicate fruits, or garlic, are best added towards the end of the fermentation or pickling process to preserve their freshness and aroma. Others, like dried spices or robust herbs, can be introduced earlier to allow their flavors to meld with the ingredients over time. Customization requires experimentation and tasting throughout the process to achieve the desired balance and taste.

In conclusion, customizing ferments and pickles is a culinary journey that celebrates individuality and creativity. It allows individuals to tailor these traditional preservation methods to their unique tastes, dietary needs, and ingredient preferences. Customization empowers home cooks and chefs to break away from standardized recipes and create dishes that resonate with their own palate. Adjusting flavor profiles, ingredient selection, and dietary considerations are all part of the customization process. It is an art that requires both knowledge and experimentation, resulting in personalized culinary creations that reflect the diverse and ever-evolving world of fermentation and pickling.

CHAPTER IX

Traditional and Cultural Variations

Fermentation Around the World

Fermentation is a culinary and cultural phenomenon that spans the globe, transcending borders, traditions, and time. This ancient preservation method, which relies on the transformative power of microorganisms, has played a pivotal role in the evolution of human diets and gastronomy. From Korean kimchi to Indian dosa, from European sauerkraut to African injera, the art of fermentation has given rise to an astonishing diversity of flavors, textures, and culinary traditions. This section explores the rich tapestry of fermentation practices worldwide, highlighting the significance of fermentation in different cultures, the variety of fermented foods and beverages, and the role of tradition and innovation in shaping these global culinary treasures.

The significance of fermentation in different cultures is deeply rooted in history, geography, and tradition. Each culture has harnessed the power of fermentation to preserve and enhance the flavors of locally available ingredients. Moreover, fermentation has often been intertwined with religious, social, and familial customs, making it an integral part of cultural identity. In some societies, fermented foods hold a sacred place and are used in rituals and celebrations. For example, in Japan, the annual sake brewing festival is a spiritual event that pays homage to the deities of rice and fermentation.

The variety of fermented foods and beverages across cultures is staggering. In Asia, the art of fermentation is exemplified by the diversity of soy-based products like miso, soy sauce, and tempeh. Korean cuisine is celebrated for its array of fermented side dishes, including the iconic kimchi. India's rich tapestry of fermented foods includes dosa, idli, and pickles, each with its own regional variations. In the Middle East, yogurt is a staple that serves as both a condiment and a base for dishes like tzatziki and labneh. Europe boasts an array of fermented delights, from sauerkraut in Germany to kefir in Eastern Europe.

Fermentation has also given rise to a multitude of beverages around the world. Wine and beer, two of the most celebrated fermented beverages, have been enjoyed across cultures for centuries. In Africa, sorghum and millet are used to make traditional fermented beers like "umqombothi" in South Africa. The Middle East is known for its fermented dairy beverages, such as "ayran" and "doogh." In Asia, kombucha and kefir are gaining popularity as probiotic-rich drinks. The global reach of fermentation is perhaps most evident in the case of tea, as countries like China, Japan, India, and Morocco each have their own unique fermented tea traditions.

The role of tradition and innovation in shaping fermentation practices is a dynamic interplay that has led to the evolution of these culinary traditions. While traditional recipes and techniques have been passed down through generations, there is room for innovation and experimentation. In recent years, fermentation has experienced a resurgence of interest and creativity, with chefs and home cooks pushing the boundaries of what is possible. The fusion of traditional practices with modern sensibilities has given rise to a new wave of fermented foods and beverages that reflect the ever-changing tastes and preferences of consumers.

One striking aspect of fermentation is its ability to transform humble ingredients into culinary delights. Take, for example, the Ethiopian staple injera, a sourdough flatbread made from teff flour. Through fermentation, this simple grain is transformed into a tangy, spongy bread that serves as a staple in Ethiopian cuisine. Similarly, the transformation of milk into cheese or yogurt through fermentation elevates these basic ingredients into a world of flavors and textures.

Fermentation also plays a crucial role in food preservation, allowing communities to store seasonal ingredients for extended periods. In Scandinavian countries, the long tradition of lactic acid fermentation preserved vegetables like cabbage as sauerkraut and cucumbers as pickles, providing a source of sustenance during harsh winters. In Asian cultures, the production of soy sauce and fish sauce enabled the preservation of seafood and soybeans, ensuring a year-round supply of these essential ingredients.

The health benefits linked with fermented foods have been recognized for centuries. Fermentation lengthen the shelf life of foods and also enhances their nutritional value. The production of beneficial probiotics during fermentation can support gut health and aid digestion. In addition, the process of fermentation can break down certain antinutrients and make nutrients more bioavailable, enhancing the nutritional content of the final product.

In conclusion, fermentation is a global culinary treasure that transcends borders, cultures, and time. Its significance in different cultures, the vast array of fermented foods and beverages, and the interplay of tradition and innovation all contribute to the richness of this culinary tradition. From kimchi in Korea to sauerkraut in Germany, from miso in Japan to injera in Ethiopia, fermentation is a testament to the human capacity for creativity, adaptability, and ingenuity in transforming humble ingredients into gastronomic delights. It is a celebration of diversity and a reminder of the shared joy of discovering new flavors and traditions from around the world.

Regional Pickling Traditions

Regional pickling traditions are a testament to the rich tapestry of culinary diversity that spans the globe. Pickling, a method of preserving food through the use of acids like vinegar or brine, has been practiced for centuries in various cultures. Each region has its distinct approach to pickling, influenced by local ingredients, climate, and cultural preferences. From the spicy pickles of the Middle East to the sweet bread and butter pickles of North America, these traditions not only ensure food preservation but also offer a spectrum of flavors, textures, and culinary customs. This section delves into the significance of regional pickling traditions, the diversity of pickled ingredients, and the cultural and culinary implications of these practices.

The significance of regional pickling traditions goes beyond mere food preservation. It is a reflection of the relationship between people and their environment. Local ingredients, often shaped by climate and geography, play a central role in dictating the types of vegetables, fruits, and even fish that are commonly pickled. For example, the pickling of cucumbers is prevalent in North America due to the abundance of this vegetable, while in Japan, pickled plums or "umeboshi" are cherished for their unique tartness and medicinal properties. The use of regional ingredients not only defines the pickling tradition but also showcases the resourcefulness of communities in making the most of their surroundings.

The diversity of pickled ingredients is a hallmark of regional pickling traditions. Each culture has its own repertoire of vegetables, fruits, and even animal products that are pickled to perfection. In the Middle East, pickled turnips and peppers add a fiery kick to meals, while in South Korea, radishes and napa cabbage are transformed into the iconic kimchi. Japan boasts a wide variety of pickled vegetables, from cucumbers to eggplants and even cherry blossoms. The choice of ingredients not only provides variety in flavor and texture but also offers a glimpse into the culinary heritage and agricultural practices of each region.

Cultural and culinary implications are intertwined with regional pickling traditions. These traditions often become an integral part of a culture's culinary identity, shaping not only what people eat but also how they eat. For instance, in the southern United States, bread and butter pickles are a quintessential accompaniment to fried chicken and other comfort foods. In contrast, the pickled vegetables of the Mediterranean, such as olives and capers, are essential components of the region's signature dishes like Greek salads and tapenades. The incorporation of pickled ingredients into daily meals speaks to the cultural significance of these traditions and their role in defining regional cuisine.

The techniques and flavor profiles associated with regional pickling traditions are as diverse as the ingredients themselves. In the Middle East, pickling often involves the use of ingredients like garlic, chili peppers, and aromatic spices, resulting in boldly flavored and spicy pickles. The Mediterranean region is known for its brine-cured olives, which can range from buttery and mild to intensely salty and briny. In Asia, fermentation plays a significant role in pickling, with methods like lacto-fermentation producing tangy and complex flavors. North America offers a wide range of pickles, from the sweet and crunchy bread and butter pickles to the robustly flavored dill pickles.

The preservation of regional pickling traditions is essential for preserving cultural heritage and culinary diversity. In a globalized world where food trends can often overshadow traditional practices, these pickling traditions serve as a link to the past and a source of pride for communities. Efforts to document and preserve these traditions, along with the knowledge and techniques associated with them, are crucial for ensuring their continued existence. Additionally, sharing these traditions with new generations through culinary education and cultural festivals helps perpetuate the appreciation of pickling as a valuable culinary art.

In conclusion, regional pickling traditions are a testament to the rich and diverse world of culinary heritage. They reflect the relationship between people, their environment, and their food, showcasing the resourcefulness of communities in preserving local ingredients. The diversity of pickled ingredients, cultural and culinary implications, and unique flavor profiles contribute to the richness of these traditions. By preserving and celebrating regional pickling practices, we not only honor the past but also ensure that the flavors and traditions of our ancestors continue to enrich our culinary experiences.

Learning from Time-Honored Techniques

Learning from time-honored techniques is a journey into the wisdom of our culinary ancestors, who mastered the art of food preservation and flavor enhancement through methods that have stood the test of time. These techniques, passed down through generations, have shaped the way we prepare and savor our meals. From fermenting vegetables to curing meats, from pickling fruits to aging cheeses, the lessons learned from these age-old practices continue to enrich our understanding of food and its transformative possibilities. This section explores the significance of learning from time-honored techniques, the enduring relevance of these methods, and the ways in which they inspire innovation and creativity in modern gastronomy.

The significance of learning from time-honored techniques lies in the preservation of culinary heritage and the wisdom of our ancestors. These techniques were born out of necessity, as early societies sought ways to extend the shelf life of food, make use of seasonal abundance, and create flavors that could be enjoyed year-round. As a result, the methods developed were not only practical but also deeply rooted in tradition. Learning from these techniques allows us to connect with the culinary history of our cultures and appreciate the resourcefulness of those who came before us.

One of the enduring lessons from time-honored techniques is the value of patience and time in culinary endeavors. Many traditional methods, such as fermentation, curing, and aging, require weeks, months, or even years to achieve the desired results. These techniques teach us the importance of allowing flavors to develop and evolve over time. For example, the aging of cheese imparts complexity and depth of flavor that cannot be rushed. Similarly, the fermentation of sauerkraut or kimchi transforms humble vegetables into tangy, probiotic-rich delicacies through the slow action of beneficial microorganisms.

The enduring relevance of time-honored techniques is evident in their continued use and adaptation in modern gastronomy. While these methods were born out of necessity, they have found a place in contemporary kitchens as chefs and home cooks alike recognize their value in enhancing flavor and preserving food. The revival of artisanal techniques, such as sourdough bread baking and craft beer brewing, reflects a renewed appreciation for the time-tested methods of our culinary heritage. Additionally, the incorporation of traditional pickling and preserving techniques into modern dishes adds depth and complexity to contemporary cuisine.

Learning from time-honored techniques also inspires innovation and creativity in the culinary world. Chefs and food enthusiasts draw inspiration from these methods to create new and exciting dishes that pay homage to tradition while embracing contemporary sensibilities. For example, the use of barrel aging, a technique historically associated with spirits and wines, has been adapted to age cocktails, hot sauces, and even coffee. The result is a fusion of old and new, where the flavors of tradition meet the innovations of the present.

Furthermore, the principles behind time-honored techniques provide a foundation for understanding and experimenting with food. Whether it's the science of fermentation, the art of preserving through salt and acid, or the craftsmanship of aging, these techniques offer valuable insights into the transformation of ingredients. This knowledge empowers chefs and home cooks to explore and push the boundaries of culinary creativity. It encourages experimentation with new flavor combinations, ingredient pairings, and preservation methods, ultimately leading to the development of unique and memorable dishes.

One example of this innovation is the resurgence of interest in heirloom and heritage ingredients. These varieties of fruits, vegetables, and grains were once staples in traditional cuisines but fell out of favor with the rise of modern agriculture. Today, chefs and food enthusiasts are rediscovering the unique flavors and characteristics of these heirloom ingredients, often using time-honored techniques to highlight their qualities. This movement not only celebrates biodiversity but also revives traditional farming practices and flavors.

In conclusion, learning from time-honored techniques is a journey of culinary discovery and appreciation. These methods, rooted in tradition and wisdom, continue to enrich our understanding of food preservation and flavor enhancement. They teach us the value of patience and time in the culinary process, inspiring innovation and creativity in modern gastronomy. By embracing the lessons of our culinary ancestors, we not only honor tradition but also pave the way for the future of food, where the flavors of the past merge with the innovations of the present.

CHAPTER X

Troubleshooting and FAQs

Common Problems and How to Fix Them

Common problems in pickling and fermenting can be frustrating but are also opportunities for learning and improvement in these age-old preservation methods. Whether you are dealing with mold growth, overly salty brine, or mushy vegetables, understanding the underlying causes of these issues and knowing how to fix them is essential for successful pickling and fermenting. This section will explore some of the most common problems encountered in these processes and provide practical solutions to address them, ensuring that your pickled and fermented creations turn out delicious and safe to eat.

One common issue in pickling and fermenting is mold growth on the surface of the brine or vegetables. Mold can develop when the brine is not adequately covering the vegetables or when the environment is not properly sanitized. To prevent mold, ensure that all vegetables are fully submerged in the brine, use clean and sterilized containers, and maintain a proper temperature for fermentation. If mold does appear, remove the affected parts, skim off the surface, and discard them. Additionally, you can add a layer of oil or a clean, sanitized weight to create a barrier between the brine and air to prevent further mold growth.

Another challenge is overly salty brine, which can make your pickles or ferments too salty to enjoy. To address this issue, you can dilute the brine by adding more water to reduce the salt concentration. Be cautious when doing this, as adding too much water can lead to spoilage. Alternatively, you can prepare a new brine solution with the correct salt-to-water ratio and transfer your vegetables to the new solution. Remember to taste and adjust the brine to your liking before transferring.

Mushy vegetables are a common problem in pickling and fermenting, often resulting from overfermentation or incorrect temperature conditions. To prevent mushiness, follow the recommended fermentation times and temperatures for the specific vegetables you are pickling. If you encounter mushy vegetables, remove them from the brine immediately to prevent further deterioration. You can also try shorter fermentation times for future batches or adjust the temperature to slow down the fermentation process.

Cloudy or hazy brine is another issue that can affect the visual appeal of your pickles or ferments. Cloudiness is often caused by the presence of yeast or lactic acid bacteria, which are natural components of fermentation. While it does not necessarily indicate spoilage, many prefer clear brine for aesthetic reasons. To clarify the brine, you can skim off any surface scum, use a clean and sanitized container, and ensure that the vegetables are submerged in the brine to prevent exposure to air. Additionally, you can utilize a clean cloth or coffee filter to strain the brine before transferring it to a storage container.

Undesired texture changes can occur in pickling and fermenting, such as vegetables becoming too soft or too crunchy. These issues can be attributed to variations in factors like vegetable freshness, temperature, and brine composition. To control texture, use fresh and firm vegetables, maintain consistent fermentation temperatures, and follow recipes that specify the desired texture. For example, if you prefer crunchy pickles, opt for recipes that specify a shorter fermentation time.

Inconsistent fermentation can lead to uneven flavors and textures in your pickled or fermented foods. This problem can arise from variations in vegetable size, temperature fluctuations, or inadequate brine coverage. To ensure consistent fermentation, aim for uniform vegetable sizes to promote even fermentation, use temperature- controlled environments when possible, and ensure that all vegetables are fully submerged in the brine. Regularly check on your fermenting batches to identify any variations and make adjustments as needed.

Overly pungent or sour flavors can be an issue, especially if your pickles or ferments turn out too intense for your taste. To mitigate this problem, you can try reducing the fermentation time for future batches to achieve a milder flavor. Additionally, using less salt in the brine or adjusting the brine composition can result in a less intense flavor. Keep in mind that personal taste preferences vary, so experimentation may be necessary to find the right balance for your palate.

Lastly, safety concerns are critical in pickling and fermenting. While many fermented foods are safe to consume, it's necessary to be aware of potential risks, such as botulism in improperly canned goods or mold contamination. To ensure safety, follow established recipes and guidelines for fermentation, use clean and sanitized equipment, and be vigilant for any signs of spoilage. If you have doubts about the safety of a batch, it's best to err on the side of caution and discard it.

In conclusion, common problems in pickling and fermenting can be discussed with a combination of knowledge, careful observation, and adjustments to your techniques. Comprehending with the underlying causes of these issues and knowing the way to fix them is essential for successful and enjoyable pickled and fermented foods. By following best practices, maintaining cleanliness, and staying vigilant during the fermentation process, you can troubleshoot and prevent common problems, ensuring that your pickles and ferments turn out delicious and safe to eat.

Answers to Frequently Asked Questions

Frequently Asked Questions (FAQs) in pickling and fermenting are essential for both beginners and experienced practitioners of these time-honored food preservation techniques. Whether you're new to the world of pickling and fermenting or looking to refine your skills, having answers to common questions can be a valuable resource. This section aims to provide comprehensive answers to frequently asked questions in pickling and fermenting, covering topics such as the difference between pickling and fermenting, safety concerns, troubleshooting, and creative variations.

What is the Difference Between Pickling and Fermenting?

Pickling and fermenting are both methods of food preservation, but they differ in their processes and outcomes. Pickling involves immersing food in a vinegar or brine solution to preserve it and create a tart, acidic flavor. Fermenting, on the other hand, relies on the action of beneficial microorganisms to transform sugars and starches in food into acids and alcohol, resulting in a tangy or sour taste. While pickling often uses vinegar as a preservative, fermenting relies on natural fermentation.

Is It Safe to Eat Fermented Foods?

Fermented foods are generally safe to eat when prepared and stored correctly. The natural fermentation procedure produces beneficial probiotics that can help in digestion and contribute to gut health. However, it's essential to follow proper fermentation practices, including cleanliness and sanitation, to prevent spoilage or harmful bacterial growth. If you have concerns about the safety of a ferment, trust your senses; if something smells or looks off, it's best to discard it.

What Equipment Do I Need for Pickling and Fermenting?

Basic equipment for pickling and fermenting includes glass or food-grade plastic containers, lids, weights, and a clean work area. For fermenting, consider using fermentation weights or airlocks to create an anaerobic environment that prevents mold growth. Additionally, a kitchen scale, measuring cups, and pH strips or meters can be helpful tools for precision in your recipes.

How Do I Troubleshoot Common Problems in Fermenting?

Common issues in fermenting, such as mold growth, overly salty brine, or mushy vegetables, can often be resolved with adjustments to your process. For example, if you encounter mold, remove affected parts, skim the surface, and ensure proper submersion in the brine. If your brine is too salty, dilute it with water or prepare a new brine solution. To address mushy vegetables, reduce fermentation time or adjust temperature conditions. For cloudy brine, skim off surface scum and strain the brine before transferring.

What Creative Variations Can I Explore in Pickling and Fermenting?

Pickling and fermenting offer endless possibilities for creative exploration. Experiment with different vegetables, fruits, herbs, and spices to create unique flavors. Consider adding garlic, chili peppers, or aromatic spices to your brine for added complexity. Explore variations like kimchi, kombucha, or lacto-fermented hot sauces to broaden your fermenting horizons. The key is to have fun and embrace the opportunity for culinary innovation.

How Long Can I Store Pickled and Fermented Foods?

The shelf life of pickled and fermented foods depends on factors like acidity, brine concentration, and storage conditions. High-acid pickles, such as vinegar-pickled cucumbers, can last for several months to a year or more when stored in a cool, dark place. Fermented foods, like sauerkraut and kimchi, can continue to develop flavor over time and may be safe to consume for several months to years when stored properly. Pickled and fermented foods should always be kept in a cool, dark pantry or the refrigerator in airtight containers.

Can I Use Store-Bought Vinegar for Pickling?

Store-bought vinegar is suitable for pickling, but it's essential to select the right type for your recipe. Common choices include white vinegar, apple cider vinegar, and rice vinegar. Ensure that the vinegar you choose has the appropriate acidity level, usually around 5% acidity, to safely pickle vegetables. Some specialty vinegars, such as malt vinegar or wine vinegar, can add unique flavors to your pickles.

Are There Any Health Advantages to Consuming Fermented Foods?

Consuming fermented foods can offer potential health benefits due to their probiotic content. Probiotics are beneficial microorganisms that can assist in supporting gut health and aid digestion. They may also contribute to a balanced gut microbiome, which is linked to overall well-being. However, the specific health benefits can vary depending on the type and quantity of fermented foods consumed. Fermented foods can be a useful addition to support digestive health when included in a balanced diet.

Can I Utilize Sea Salt or Kosher Salt for Pickling and Fermenting?

Sea salt and kosher salt are acceptable choices for pickling and fermenting, provided they do not contain additives like anti-caking agents or iodine. These additives can hinder with the fermentation process. When using sea salt or kosher salt in pickling or fermenting recipes, be sure to measure by weight, as the crystal sizes can vary. Table salt, which is finely ground and may contain additives, is generally not recommended for these processes.

How Do I Know When My Ferment is Ready to Eat?

The readiness of a ferment depends on personal preference and the recipe. Taste your ferment periodically to assess its flavor and texture. When it reaches the desired level of tartness or sourness, and the texture is to your liking, it is ready to eat. Some ferments, like sauerkraut, may continue to develop flavor over time. Put your ferment in the fridge to halt the fermenting process and preserve its quality once it's ready.

In conclusion, understanding and addressing frequently asked questions in pickling and fermenting are essential for successful and enjoyable food preservation and flavor enhancement. Whether you're navigating the differences between pickling and fermenting, troubleshooting common problems, or exploring creative variations, having the knowledge and resources to do so can enhance your culinary experiences. By following best practices, staying curious, and embracing the wisdom of experienced practitioners, you can embark on a rewarding journey of pickling and fermenting with confidence and creativity.

CHAPTER XI

Beyond the Basics

Scaling Up Production

Scaling up production in pickling and fermenting is a natural progression for individuals who have mastered the art of these preservation techniques and are looking to share their creations with a larger audience. Whether you're a home enthusiast ready to turn your hobby into a small business or a chef aiming to incorporate pickled and fermented products into your restaurant's menu, scaling up production requires careful planning, increased efficiency, and adherence to food safety regulations. This section navigates the key considerations and steps involved in expanding production capacity for pickling and fermenting, including sourcing ingredients, equipment selection, production methods, quality control, and market strategies.

One of the initial challenges when scaling up production is sourcing a consistent and reliable supply of ingredients. For pickling and fermenting, the quality of the ingredients is paramount. Seek out local farmers and suppliers who can provide fresh and high-quality vegetables, fruits, and other ingredients required for your recipes. Establishing strong relationships with these suppliers can ensure a steady and consistent source of raw materials as your production grows.

Selecting the right equipment is crucial to increasing production efficiency. As the scale of production increases, it may become impractical to rely solely on small-scale, home kitchen equipment. Consider investing in larger fermentation vessels, commercial-grade stainless steel containers, and specialized equipment like vegetable washers, slicers, and packagers. These investments can streamline the production process and improve the consistency as well as the quality of your products.

Production methods play a significant role in scaling up successfully. Adapt your recipes and processes to accommodate larger batch sizes while maintaining the integrity of your pickles and ferments. Implement standardized procedures and quality control measures to ensure that every batch meets your desired flavor and texture profiles. Additionally, consider automation and mechanization options to increase production efficiency while reducing labor costs.

Maintaining consistent quality is essential when scaling up production in pickling and fermenting. Establish stringent quality control measures to monitor the entire production process, from ingredient preparation to fermentation and packaging. Regularly test the pH levels and taste samples to guarantee that the flavors and textures meet your standards. Implement strict sanitation practices to prevent contamination and spoilage. Quality control is paramount to building and maintaining a positive reputation for your products.

Compliance with the food safety regulations is non-negotiable when scaling up production. Familiarize yourself with the local, state, and federal food safety regulations and ensure that your production facility and processes meet all requirements. This may involve obtaining necessary permits, putting in place Hazard Analysis and Critical Control Points (also called HACCP) plans, and conducting regular inspections. Prioritize food safety to protect both your customers and your business.

Scaling up production also necessitates careful consideration of storage and distribution. As your inventory grows, you'll need adequate storage facilities to maintain product quality. Invest in temperature- controlled storage to extend the shelf life of your pickled and fermented products. Develop a distribution strategy that includes packaging, labeling, and delivery methods. Consider working with local markets, restaurants, or online platforms to reach a wider customer base.

Market strategies are crucial for successfully introducing your expanded line of pickled and fermented products to a broader audience. Develop a clear brand identity and story that communicates the uniqueness and quality of your offerings. Consider participating in farmers' markets, food festivals, or trade shows to showcase your products and also connect with potential customers. Create an online presence via website or a social media to achieve a broader audience and facilitate online sales.

Pricing your products appropriately is a critical aspect of your market strategy. Take into account the costs of ingredients, production, labor, and overhead when determining pricing. Research the market to have a knowledge the price range for similar products and position your offerings competitively. Consider offering various package sizes to cater to different customer preferences and budgets.

To increase awareness of a brand and draw in customers, marketing and advertising must be done well. Create a marketing strategy incorporating both online and offline platforms. Utilize email marketing, content marketing, as well as social media to interact with your audience and tell the tale of your pickling and fermentation process. Consider collaborating with local chefs or food influencers to create buzz around your products.

When scaling up production, it's essential to remain adaptable and open to feedback. Listen to customer feedback and adjust your recipes or processes accordingly. Continuously improve and refine your products based on customer preferences and market trends. Building a loyal customer base requires a commitment to quality and a willingness to evolve.

In conclusion, scaling up production in pickling and fermenting is a rewarding endeavor that requires careful planning, attention to quality, and adherence to food safety regulations. By sourcing quality ingredients, selecting the right equipment, optimizing production methods, and maintaining stringent quality control, you can successfully expand your production capacity. Additionally, developing effective market strategies, pricing your products competitively, and prioritizing marketing and promotion are essential for achieving a wider audience and building a successful pickling and fermenting business. As you embark on this journey, remember that adaptability and a commitment to constant improvement are key to long-term success in the world of pickling and fermenting.

Starting a Fermentation or Pickling Business

Starting a fermentation or pickling business is an exciting venture that enable you to turn your passion for preserving and flavor enhancement into a profitable enterprise. Whether you're a seasoned home fermenter looking to share your creations with a wider audience or a culinary enthusiast with a unique product idea, launching a fermentation or pickling business requires careful planning, a deep understanding of the craft, and a commitment to quality. This section will navigate the key steps and considerations involved in starting and running a successful fermentation or pickling business, from product development and production to marketing and distribution.

Product Development and Recipe Refinement: The foundation of any successful fermentation or pickling business is exceptional products with distinctive flavors.

Begin by developing your recipes, experimenting with different ingredients, spices, and fermentation times to create unique and appealing offerings. Pay close attention to the balance of flavors, texture, and acidity to ensure that your products stand out in the market. Recipe refinement is an ongoing process, so be open to feedback and continually strive to enhance your creations.

Market Research and Target Audience: Prior launching your business, conduct thorough market research to determine your target audience and examine the demand for your products. Consider factors such as demographics, consumer preferences, and market trends. Determine whether your focus will be on a niche market, such as artisanal fermented hot sauces, or a broader audience interested in a variety of fermented and pickled goods. Understanding your potential customers is essential for tailoring your products and marketing strategies.

Business Plan and Legal Requirements: Develop a comprehensive business plan that outlines your business strategies, goals, and financial projections. Consider factors such as startup costs, production expenses, pricing strategies, and revenue forecasts. Ensure that your business complies with every legal requirements, including permits, licenses, and food safety regulations. Consult with local health authorities and regulatory agencies to understand the certain regulations that apply to your fermentation or pickling business.

Production Facility and Equipment: Choose a suitable production facility equipped with the necessary equipment for your operations. The facility should meet food safety standards and allow for efficient production processes. Invest in high-quality equipment, such as fermentation vessels, food processors, packaging machines, and storage facilities. Ensure that your production area is clean, organized, and optimized for food safety practices.

Quality Control and Food Safety: Maintain strict quality control measures to guarantee the consistency as well as the safety of your products. Implement Hazard Analysis and Critical Control Points (also called HACCP) plans to identify potential hazards and establish preventive measures. Regularly test pH levels and conduct sensory evaluations to monitor product quality. Develop sanitation protocols and procedures to prevent contamination and spoilage. Prioritize food safety to safeguard your customers and build trust in your brand.

Packaging and Labeling: Design attractive and informative packaging that reflects the quality and identity of your products. Consider eco-friendly and sustainable packaging options to align with consumer preferences. Ensure that your labels comply with regulatory requirements, including ingredient lists, nutrition facts, allergen information, and proper labeling of fermented or pickled goods. Effective packaging and labeling contribute to your product's shelf appeal and consumer trust.

Marketing and Branding: Establish a distinctive brand identity that appeals to your intended market. Create a captivating brand narrative that conveys your love of pickling or fermentation as well as the distinctiveness of your goods. Make use of both online and offline marketing techniques, such as influencer or chef partnerships, email marketing, content marketing, and social media. To showcase your items to prospective buyers, go to trade exhibitions, farmers' markets, and culinary festivals in your area. Developing loyal customers and brand recognition are critical to your company's success.

Distribution and Sales Channels: Consider your distribution strategy, including sales channels and partnerships. Explore options such as online sales through your website or e-commerce platforms, wholesale distribution to local retailers, or collaborations with restaurants and specialty stores. Choose distribution channels that are in line with your target audience and business goals. Efficient logistics and reliable delivery methods are crucial for timely and safe product distribution.

Financial Management and Sustainability: Manage your finances prudently to ensure the sustainability and growth of your business. Keep accurate records of expenses, revenues, and profit margins. Monitor your cash flow and budget effectively to cover operational costs and investments. Consider reinvesting profits into business expansion, product development, or marketing initiatives. Financial stability is necessary for the long-term success of your fermentation or pickling business.

Customer Engagement and Feedback: Engage with your customers and encourage feedback to build relationships and improve your products. Create opportunities for customer interaction, such as tastings, workshops, or online communities dedicated to fermentation and pickling enthusiasts. Listen to customer suggestions and concerns, and use their feedback to refine your recipes and offerings. Building a loyal customer foundation is crucial for the growth and sustainability of your business.

Scaling Up and Innovation: As your fermentation or pickling business grows, explore opportunities for scaling up production and expanding your product line. Invest in additional equipment and production facilities to meet increased demand. Continuously innovate by introducing new flavors, variations, or limited-edition releases to keep your product offerings exciting and fresh. Embrace new trends and emerging ingredients to stay competitive in the market.

In conclusion, starting a fermentation or pickling business is a rewarding journey that combines culinary passion with entrepreneurship. By focusing on product development, market research, legal compliance, quality control, branding, and effective distribution, you can create a thriving business that offers unique and delicious fermented and pickled goods to a growing customer base. As you embark on this entrepreneurial endeavor, remember that dedication, creativity, and a commitment to quality are key ingredients for success in the world of fermentation and pickling.

Advanced Techniques and Ideas

In the realm of fermentation and pickling businesses, mastering advanced techniques and embracing innovative ideas can set your enterprise apart, allowing you to create distinctive and sought-after products. Whether you're an established business owner looking to elevate your offerings or an aspiring entrepreneur eager to explore new horizons, this section delves into advanced techniques and creative concepts that can propel your fermentation or pickling business to the next level.

Exploring Unique Fermentation and Pickling Techniques: Advanced techniques in fermentation and pickling open up a world of possibilities for crafting exceptional products. Consider delving into techniques such as barrel aging, where your ferments or pickles are aged in wooden barrels to impart complex flavors and aromas. Experiment with different fermentation vessels, like ceramic crocks or clay pots, to influence the microbial communities and flavors of your products. Explore controlled wild fermentation, where you harness naturally occurring microbes from specific environments to create unique flavors.

Blending Traditional and Modern Approaches: Combining traditional methods with modern technology can yield remarkable results in the world of fermentation and pickling. For example, traditional kimchi recipes can benefit from precise temperature and humidity control in fermentation chambers. Utilize pH meters and digital thermometers to monitor and maintain optimal conditions. Additionally, consider implementing data logging and analysis tools to track the progress of your ferments, allowing for data-driven improvements and consistency.

Flavor Pairing and Fusion Creations: Innovation in flavor pairing and fusion is a captivating avenue to explore. Experiment with combining diverse ingredients to create intriguing flavor profiles. For instance, infuse traditional sauerkraut with Asian-inspired flavors by incorporating ingredients like ginger, sesame, and miso. Embrace culinary creativity by fusing international cuisines, such as fermenting Mexican-inspired pickles with Middle Eastern spices. The fusion of flavors can captivate adventurous palates and broaden your product range.

Limited Edition and Seasonal Offerings: Introduce limited edition and seasonal offerings to entice customers with exclusivity and freshness. Craft small-batch releases that showcase rare or seasonal ingredients. For example, create a limited edition pickle featuring heirloom vegetables only available during specific times of the year. Highlight the seasonal charm of your products through themed packaging and marketing campaigns, building anticipation among your customer base.

Collaborations and Guest Fermenters: Collaborations with other food artisans, chefs, or guest fermenters can inject fresh perspectives into your product line. Partner with local chefs to co-create unique pickles or ferments that align with their culinary expertise. Invite guest fermenters to lead workshops or create limited-run products, offering customers a taste of different fermentation styles and traditions. Collaborations can broaden your network and introduce your brand to new audiences.

Artisanal Presentation and Packaging: Elevate the visual appeal of your products through artisanal presentation and packaging. Consider hand-labeling jars with artistic flair or using handcrafted wooden lids for a rustic touch. Embrace sustainable packaging options that resonate with eco-conscious consumers. The presentation of your products is an opportunity to convey craftsmanship and attention to detail, leaving a lasting impression.

Interactive Customer Experiences: Engage customers with interactive experiences that connect them with the art of fermentation and pickling. Host fermentation workshops or pickle-making classes to educate and inspire enthusiasts. Create tasting events where customers can sample a variety of your products and gain a deeper appreciation for their complexity. Creating a community around your business can encourage enthusiasm and loyalty from your customers.

Exploring Novel Ingredients and Techniques: Stay at the forefront of innovation by exploring novel ingredients and techniques. Experiment with unconventional vegetables, fruits, or grains to create entirely new products. Dive into the world of fermentation byproducts like vinegar, kombucha, or kefir, offering a diverse range of offerings to cater to different tastes. Embrace fermentation with emerging superfoods or health-focused ingredients to tap into health-conscious markets.

Collaborations with Local Farmers and Foragers: Forge partnerships with local farmers and foragers to access unique and hyper-local ingredients. Collaborate with foragers to incorporate wild edibles like ramps, mushrooms, or seaweed into your pickles and ferments. Support local agriculture by sourcing heirloom varieties of vegetables and fruits that tell a regional story through your products. These collaborations can enhance the authenticity and sustainability of your offerings.

Sustainability and Zero-Waste Initiatives: Embrace sustainability and zero-waste initiatives to resonate with environmentally conscious consumers. Implement efficient waste reduction practices, such as utilizing leftover brine for other culinary purposes. Consider eco-friendly packaging options, including reusable jars or containers. Communicate your commitment to sustainability through transparent labeling and messaging, appealing to eco-minded customers.

Tapping into the Beverage Market: Explore the beverage market by fermenting unique beverages like kombucha, kefir, or shrubs (fermented fruit syrups). Craft innovative flavor profiles that stand out in the crowded beverage space. Offer non-alcoholic alternatives with complex and intriguing flavors, targeting health-conscious and adventurous consumers. Diversifying into beverages can expand your product line and customer reach.

In conclusion, advanced techniques and creative ideas can propel your fermentation or pickling business to new heights, allowing you to craft exceptional products that resonate with discerning customers. Whether you're refining traditional methods, embracing modern technology, or exploring novel flavors and collaborations, the world of fermentation and pickling offers boundless opportunities for innovation. By staying curious, staying true to your craft, and remaining open to experimentation, you can carve a unique niche in the culinary world and leave a lasting mark in the realm of fermentation and pickling.

CONCLUSION

For those enthusiastic about fermenting and pickling food for long-term storage, "Fermenting & Pickling Essentials: Time-Honored Techniques for Long-Term Storage" is an extensive and priceless resource. Readers are guided through the rich history, underlying ideas, and sophisticated skills of these ancient culinary traditions throughout the book.

The book starts by exploring the fundamentals of pickling and fermentation, providing a comprehensive grasp of the procedures involved. From there, it takes readers on a tour of various techniques and recipes, from traditional dill pickles to unique kimchi and creative fusion dishes. Every chapter serves as a doorway to a universe of tastes, textures, and inventive cooking.

This work stands out for its steadfast adherence to authenticity and tradition. It offers the ideal blend of the old and the new by honoring traditional methods and welcoming innovative advancements. The recipes celebrate the science and artistry of pickling and fermentation, not merely a set of instructions.

Finally, "Fermenting & Pickling Essentials" is an indispensable resource for novices and experts alike. It gives readers the information and abilities they need to start their own preservation adventure, from locating components to increasing output. This book is a celebration of the craftsmanship of pickling and fermenting, and it encourages readers to experiment with the countless combinations of flavors, textures, and creative culinary combinations that these methods may produce.

Thank you for buying and reading/ listening to our book. If you found this book useful/ helpful please take a few minutes and leave a review on the platform where you purchased our book. Your feedback matters greatly to us.